INVESTMENT SCHEMES, SCAMS

& STRATEGIES RETIREES SHOULD AVOID

Financial sharks prey on baby boomers: Learn how to avoid devastating losses

IRWIN G. STEIN, ESQ.

XXII Century Consulting
SAN RAFAEL, CALIFORNIA

XXII Century Consulting
454 Las Gallinas Ave, #148
San Rafael CA 94903
www.laweconomicscapital.com
Profstein18@yahoo.com

Ordering Information:
Quantity sales. Special discounts are available on quantity purchases by corporations, associations, and others. For details, contact the "Special Sales Department" at the address above.

Investment Schemes, Scams & Strategies Retirees Should Avoid/
Irwin G. Stein, Esq. -- 1st ed.
ISBN 978-0-9967435-0-1

To the doctors, and especially to the nurses and staff, at the University of California San Francisco Medical Center who provide world-class medical care, every day.

Table of Contents

Preface

In October 2011 I was diagnosed with a nasty type of leukemia. I began writing this book, using voice-activated software, while a patient at the University of California San Francisco Medical Center. Frankly, I think that the nurses were happy that I was occupying myself.

Whatever Amazon.com sends me for sales of this book, I intend to sign over to the University to support research to find cures for blood cancers.

I hope to inform retirees how to avoid making foolish mistakes with their money.

I know from personal experience that each year a great many retirees will have their retirements ruined because they dealt with the wrong financial professionals or because they purchased the wrong investments. When the markets turn down, hundreds of billions of dollars will be lost. These losses are largely avoidable.

If you are already retired, or if you have elderly parents, please know that *senior citizens are targeted in the financial markets* by dishonest financial operators who would steal their money.

Some people sell seniors investments that they know are likely to become worthless.

Many of these financial sharks look like legitimate financial professionals. Some work for the largest and most respected financial institutions.

Have a conversation about financial fraud with your parents. Or better yet, buy them a copy of this book and support cancer research.

More insidious than the out-and-out thieves are the mainstream financial firms and mainstream financial advisors who fill the marketplace with *bad information*. The *common knowledge* about retirement planning and retirement investing is skewed in the financial services industry's favor. The information that they pass along to retirees as *truth* is designed to help that industry make the most money.

The examples that I use in this book are real-life cases— actual investments that people bought or were sold, that resulted in real and substantial losses. These losses frequently changed the lives of entire families. In many of the cases, my own clients lost millions of dollars, and I only represented a small fraction of the people who had purchased these investments.

I have changed the names of some of these investments and some of the companies. I have rounded off the numbers to make the math easier so that the point I am trying to make will be more direct. Several of the *not its real name* companies are an amalgam of several firms.

In almost every case, I had the actual sales or marketing materials for the investment or firm that I was describing in front of me as I described it. I wanted to accurately reflect the *sales pitch* for these investments. The investments change and the people behind the investments change. *However, the sales pitch goes on and on with little modification because it works.*

Investors represent the capital in our capital formation system. Individual investors get little respect in the financial markets. I have witnessed investments that institutional investors refused to buy. The investments were then repackaged and sold to "sophisticated" individual investors in transactions that had little hope of success. "Packaging" investments for "sophisticated" individual investors is an industry populated by professional promoters who earn large fees for creating financial products that stockbrokers can sell.

Individual investors rarely investigate an investment before they buy it; few would truly know how to do so. Retirees especially, trust the financial professionals with whom they deal.

Every year, thousands and thousands of retirees have that trust violated because they are sold bad investments. Some may not become aware of it until years later when the investments actually fail.

Many of the retirees whom I represented in the post-2008 market downturn had the same basic investments that many of my clients had in the early 1990s, when a similar market downturn caused millions of retirees to suffer billions of dollars in losses. The names, faces and projects being financed were different, but the structure, intent and the sales pitch of these financial products were essentially the same.

Retirees are told that they can get *a dependable monthly or quarterly check at a rate several percentage points higher than they might get if they kept their money in a bank or if they invested their money in bonds.* The risks of these investments are minimized, if they are considered at all.

The US financial markets are among the most heavily regulated and are considered among the most transparent and investor-friendly financial markets in the world. Regulators, who are keenly aware of this particular problem—*high risk investments being sold to retirees*—could eliminate the problem by reducing the commission for selling these products to people over the age of 65 to zero or by taking a comparable action. It is not likely to happen.

When the market does take a downturn and the losses begin to pile up, seniors and retirees will need to be represented by knowledgeable lawyers like myself to help them recover their losses. **If you follow the advice in this book, it is likely that we will never meet, at least professionally.**

Investing is about mathematics. If you are an investor, you must understand the math and how it is correctly applied. Investments that you would consider purchasing should be reviewed and analyzed. Economic conditions in the US and other markets should be considered. If you are not doing this yourself, then you will probably want to hire someone else to handle your investments for you. Not all investment advisors are the same. Everyone wants to hire the best. Could you really find the right one for you?

This is especially true for fiduciary investors—the people who sit on the investment committees of corporate pension plans, charities and endowments. The committees are tasked with the oversight of the firm that is choosing investments for the plan or fund. If you were asked to sit on the investment committee of a charity, could you have spotted one of the many Bernie Madoffs in the marketplace?

I intend to offer my thoughts about which investments and investment strategies retirees should avoid. If you eliminate these, and the people who sell them from your purview, you will at least have a fighting chance of not making a potentially costly mistake.

Introduction

What happens to retirees in the financial markets is a national disgrace.

Retirees who have been fortunate enough to put away $500,000 or more to cover their retirement expenses know that very few of their contemporary baby boomers will have as much. A lot of books and a lot of people will offer you strategies on how to invest your money or which specific investments to buy. I intend to tell you which investments and strategies that you would do well to avoid.

I have worked as an attorney in and around the financial markets for 40 years. I have helped thousands of investors who were victims of financial fraud and inappropriate investments. Retirees have always made up a disproportionate number of my clients because they are targeted by financial fraudsters. Both the mainstream financial industry and financial scam artists see baby boomers as easy marks.

Most retirees (and most investors) purchase the investments that their brokers or advisors recommend. We acknowledge that financial professionals know more about the financial markets and about any particular investment that they are recommending than we do.

The person from whom you seek financial advice is the key person who will be responsible for determining exactly how much money you will have to spend between the time that you retire and the time that you die.

Sorting through the competition for your retirement advisor can be daunting. Despite all that is written on retirement planning, there is little good advice on how to find the right person to assist you. I hope to offer some useful information and advice based upon my own experience and the experiences of my clients.

My clients typically dealt with the wrong financial firms and the wrong financial professionals. Many purchased investments or followed strategies that caused their funds to simply evaporate within five or seven years after they retired. A great many of these people lost a significant amount of their life's savings.

Many of these people had sought out the assistance of a financial professional specifically to plan for their retirement. The investments and strategies that were presented to them sounded good but did not perform as advertised.

Many of these investments and strategies always had a high risk of failure and were never suitable investments for risk-adverse retirees. These losses were foreseeable and avoidable.

The billions upon billions of dollars of losses suffered by retirees in the financial markets were largely avoidable—and can be in the future. I said as much to the Securities and Exchange Commission (the SEC) when they asked about *investment fraud and the elderly* almost twenty years ago. (If you wish to have a copy of my 1996 submission to the SEC on this subject, send me an email and I will forward one to you.)

I suggested then that the SEC clearly label these investments in a way that indicated that they were **too risky for retirees**. Just like that, in **oversized, bold type** right above where the customer signs his/her name to make the purchase. Retirees could be educated to be skeptical of anyone who suggested that they make any investment that carries the label.

The same type of investment fraud directed at retirees that I witnessed in the 1980s and 1990s, and wrote about to the SEC in 1996, has continued unabated since that time. Millions of retirees continue to be steered into investments that are far riskier than those that they should want or need. Many are steered into investments that are out-and-out frauds.

Two truths will guide this discussion: 1) Investments and strategies that pay a higher return to investors generally have a higher risk of loss; 2) Investments and strategies that have a higher risk of loss generally pay higher commissions and fees to the financial professionals who sell them.

The entire discussion about retirement investing is skewed by the idea that you *need to have a higher return* on your money because you need to *maintain your pre-retirement lifestyle.*

Underlying the discussion is the reality that if the customers *need* a higher return, then they will necessarily be steered to financial products upon which the salespeople will earn higher commissions. This conflict causes some less scrupulous financial professionals to minimize the risks of high-risk investments in order to make a sale.

The securities industry has rules that prohibit financial professionals from recommending any investment if the customer clearly does not want to take the risk or cannot afford to sustain the loss. Not everyone in the securities industry follows the rules.

Actual portfolio construction for a *retired income investor* is neither difficult nor complicated. **If you need to draw a check from the account every month or every quarter, any competent financial professional should be able to help you to earn anywhere between 4% (with less risk) and 8% (with more**

risk) per year and to peg your return with a high degree of specificity.

If you use the services of a Registered Investment Advisor it should not cost you all that much to get it done. There are minimal fees and commissions upfront and usually about 1% to 2% per year of your portfolio's value for constant monitoring and necessary adjustments.

Every year, many retired income investors are steered into two financial products: ***private placements*** and ***variable annuities.*** The sales pitch for both focuses investors on a larger monthly check. These two products pay higher commissions than almost anything else that a stockbroker or investment advisor could sell. Brokers who sell these two products may earn several times what an advisor might earn from the same customers investing the same amount of money in a more rational, conservative fashion.

Both private placements and variable annuities are high risk and high commission investment products. Commissions and upfront fees for both of these products can exceed 10% of the funds that you are investing. The people managing the private placements and annuities pay themselves high fees every year to manage the investment. It is easy to see why the managers need to take higher risks with what is left after these fees, in an attempt to provide high returns to investors.

When the market turns down again those higher risks will come home to roost. Millions of retirees who were sold these two financial products—private placements and variable annuities—will suffer hundreds of billions of dollars in losses.

A large number of stockbrokerage firms and insurance companies sell hundreds of billions of dollars worth of these two investments every year.

Neither investment should be thought of as suitable for most seniors for three reasons: the costs are high, they require a long time to breakeven and especially because the potential for losses are great.

All over America there are stockbrokers and stockbrokerage firms that specialize in these two financial products. Many advertise that they are *retirement investment specialists*. Do not be fooled.

Retirement specialists should not ordinarily be expected to handle high-risk investments. If a person claims to be a retirement investment specialist because they offer retirees investments that pay high returns, be very, very careful.

Retirees generally do not want their retirement funds to be wiped out or anything close to it. Most of my clients did not expect to lose anything close to the losses that they actually suffered.

Many of my clients reported that they had a specific conversation with the financial professional who had sold them the offending investments. They had made it absolutely clear that they could not afford to lose this money.

Many were assured by the financial professionals that the investments they were purchasing were *safe and suitable for retirees* and more specifically, suitable investments for them.

Safe and suitable for retirees is the right idea but the investment must back up the promise. Very few investments can actually be considered to be safe for anyone.

Sometimes the salesperson said that the investment was *safe or secure* because there was real estate or other assets on the balance sheet. Sometimes the salesperson brushed off written warnings with, *"all investments have risks"* or *"that's just legal boilerplate."*

Sometimes the salesperson would say that their firm had thoroughly investigated the investment before it was offered to customers, when that was a lie. Some salespeople claimed to have put their families into the same investments or to have invested themselves, when that was a lie.

Regardless of what the printed documents say, the primary reason that people buy these investments is because *they trust the person who is selling these investments to them*. Far too often that trust is misplaced.

When the investments fail and the investors have lost a substantial amount of their retirement funds because these investments were too risky for them from the outset, they come to attorneys like me, asking for help to recover their losses.

More often than not, by the time they get to me, these retirees are like deer confronted by a car's headlights—stunned and uncertain what happened to them; uncertain what to do next.

At the time that they retired, these individuals frequently had more liquid cash than at any time before in their lives. Some had sold their home or business. Some had taken lump sums from their employee retirement plans. Most had no experience investing that much money. Few asked if it was a good time to invest at all.

Many of these people began drawing from their retirement funds every month to help cover their monthly expenses as soon as they retired or shortly thereafter. It was always reasonable to expect that their retirement investments needed to continue to provide that monthly support to them until they died and frequently longer, for a surviving spouse. It should not have been difficult for them to achieve this result.

The conversation that retirees have with the investment professional with whom they deal regarding risk and reward should leave nothing to doubt. Too many people have told me that their financial professional never told them that they could lose 70%, 80% or even 100% of the money that they were investing. In some cases, those disclosures were buried in the small print—which the financial professional, at least, should have read, understood and explained.

Finding a good, honest financial advisor can be a real problem, not because there are not enough good ones out there, but because people often fail to use some basic standards to judge their advisor or prospective advisor.

We expect our doctors, lawyers and accountants to act like *professionals* when we deal with them. There is nothing wrong with holding a financial advisor to the same standard.

Too many of the people who hold themselves out as professionals in the financial markets are salespeople—nothing more or less. The financial markets are complex and many salespeople really do not understand the markets themselves. Some salespeople do not let their lack of knowledge get in the way of making a sale.

Many retirees find a financial advisor by referral or are invited to a seminar where they believe that they are going to obtain "good" information. There is nothing wrong with either method of finding a good financial advisor, but neither should you assume that either method would necessarily yield that result.

It is not uncommon for people to do business with other people in their church or with whom they share an ethnicity or affinity. Financial fraudsters know this. Some will use that affinity to build trust and to exploit that trust for their own gain. It is common for a member of an ethnic, religious or civic group to target other members of the same group for fraudulent investment sales.

Ordained clergy of many faiths and denominations are themselves the source of a substantial amount of financial fraud around the world. Billions of dollars are siphoned off from legitimate projects sponsored by legitimate religious organizations every year.

If you wish to give your money away to your church or religious organization to support their good works, by all means do so. If the church is offering to pay you a 15%-20% return to get you to buy bonds for a construction or missionary project (or religious theme park for that matter), you need to understand that as an investment, there is a substantial risk that your money will not be returned.

What should be sobering is that these religious investment scams are not lower level employees skimming from the collection plates. They are frequently complex financial schemes where the investors' funds are diverted to pay for a pastor's lavish lifestyle.

Doctors who treat the elderly are aware that many become victims of investment fraud or financial exploitation. Studies indicate that as many as nine out of ten of the doctors and nurses who treat these patients believe that mild cognitive impairment often makes seniors more vulnerable to investment fraud or financial exploitation.

The financial services industry offers no real training for financial professionals on how to spot cognitive impairment in potential customers who are senior citizens. The general attitude of the industry towards seniors is that if they have money and want to invest, then the organized financial services industry is here to assist them.

The financial services industry is built upon obtaining the consumers' trust. When the investments fail, it is this feeling of a *breach of trust* that really makes people angry.

This book is intended to help you avoid the wrong advisors and the wrong investments. You should avoid them because they sell financial products and strategies that are doomed to fail. Failure means that as you get older you will be a lot closer to being broke.

The companies that are most active selling investments to retirees are judged by how much money they make on their bottom line, not how much money the retirees make.

The financial services industry is the source of much of the misinformation about retirement planning and retirement investing. That misinformation skews the conversation about investing retirement funds and has become embedded in the mainstream mindset.

In the process of researching this book, I searched many websites and publications from government agencies and respected consumer groups. Some of those publications quoted statistics that are unsupported by relevant data. Others make assumptions about retirement living based upon how a prior generation lived.

This misinformation permeates the marketplace. It helps the financial services industry make a great deal of money. At the same time, it causes many retirees to take unnecessary investment risks and to suffer unnecessary losses.

Much of the advice that I offer in this book will be hard to find elsewhere. Many of the questions that I ask, or that I suggest that you ask, do not appear in other publications or on other experts' lists. My take on all this comes from a different perspective.

The financial services industry looks upon the hundreds of billions of dollars that baby boomers will invest in the next twenty years as its greatest prize. Baby boomers and retirees need to be very careful with their money.

Post-retirement investing is not that complicated. For most people it is absolutely essential that they get it right. For everyone, it should be absolutely essential that they do not get it very wrong.

Much of this book will cover specific investments that were sold to retirees which were far too risky or which were out-and-out scams. Almost all were sold to those retirees by licensed stockbrokers or Registered Investment Advisors. Most of the salespeople were well paid for making the offending sales.

I will try to replicate the sales pitch for these various investments. In most cases what you hear and what you get are not the same.

I have brought claims against hundreds of stockbrokers, financial planners and Registered Investment Advisors who had sold retirees investments that simply evaporated. I believe that the average retired person who is looking to invest a significant amount of money is a sitting duck waiting to be taken.

Notwithstanding, I would still urge you to find a competent, honest financial professional to help you create, manage and maintain an investment portfolio both before and after you retire. I will discuss how you might find one in some detail in a later chapter.

CHAPTER I

Retirement Planning and Investing: One Man's Approach

A great deal of retirement planning and investing is based in mathematics. A great many people who advise retirees about investments cannot themselves do the math correctly. Much of what passes for mainstream retirement planning uses math that is specifically designed to direct retirees into investments that will generate the most money for the financial services industry.

Many people view retirement planning as answering the question: how will I pay my bills after I stop working? You can make it as simple or as complicated as you like. Like anything else in life, a little common sense can go a long way.

As an attorney and as a cancer patient, I will tell you that one thing that you should consider as you plan for your retirement is the end of your retirement, what is properly called *planning to die*. Visit an attorney and put your affairs in order. Update your will, execute your trusts and take care of your charitable donations. Speak with the person who handles your taxes. A little bit of tax planning can save you and your heirs thousands of dollars.

You will not know when you might have a heart attack or get struck down by a drunk driver. I woke up one morning with a stomachache and three hours later they told me it was leukemia.

Take care of the people who will be taking care of you. Have *the conversation* with those you love about your care and your wishes for the end of your life. Sign a healthcare directive. Get all of the paperwork that you may need later, out of the way now.

If you are going to take the time and put in the thought to properly plan for your retirement—and it takes both—you should consider hiring a *certified financial planner* to help you. I am always amazed when a client tells me that they hired a wedding planner for their daughter's wedding, which essentially covered one weekend of activities, but did not hire a financial planner to help them plan for the activities that would define the rest of their lives after they retired.

Financial planners who have the designation CFP® or ChFC® are specially trained to help you plan for your retirement correctly. They are specifically required to take courses on *ethics.*

A good financial planner will work for an hourly fee. They will help you take a financial inventory of what you have and will help you to take a realistic look at your expenses and income going forward into retirement.

You can judge a good financial planner by how much time they spend asking questions and *getting to know you, your family and your current situation.*

What does my retirement plan look like? My personal financial plan is not so much an investment plan as a budget for living after I retire. I expect to keep working for a few years past age 65 so that when I eventually file for Social Security my monthly checks will be a little larger. At the same time I am funding my retirement accounts with a much as I can.

I recently paid off my mortgage and I am accumulating some of that money each month in a savings account. When I do retire I expect the savings account to provide enough of a reserve to cover normal contingencies and expenses like a new car every few years or a new roof or water heater if I need one. The savings account will also be available for some of the increased medical and living expenses that I may have as I get older.

When I became ill, I moved the bulk of my retirement account into income-producing investments. I was 61 at the time and I was able to invest most to it to yield about 6.5%.

At the time, I expected to continue to work until I was at least 67 or 68. The cumulative effect of adding the income to the account each year and reinvesting it will mean that I will have about 35% more in the account when I finally do begin drawing on it. Each monthly check will be that much larger.

My initial retirement budget tells me that I should have enough income every month to cover my monthly expenses first, and then have enough left over so that I can visit my kids and enjoy myself. I am going to be *retired*. The investments that I have should continue to provide income for as long as I live and beyond, for my family, when I die.

My budget also acknowledges that should my cancer relapse, the money that I had earmarked for travel and entertainment will likely be spent on prescriptions, co-pays and other health care. It is that flexibility that tells me that *my plan will work for my life.*

Sound simple? It is and for me, at least, it is a good retirement plan and one with which I am very comfortable. I would think that most people would want a fairly simple plan as well.

Most retirement plans focus on the first ten years after you retire when you can have the most realistic idea of what your lifestyle might be like. Most retirement plans assume that your lifestyle will be the same no matter how old that you get.

Whether or not you will need long-term care and for how long is much more likely to impact your retirement lifestyle and retirement finances than anything else. Many retirees consider long-term care insurance but you will only have a conversation about it if the financial professional whom you consult has an appropriate license to sell it to you.

A good retirement plan should ask the question: ***What will my expenses be after I retire and looking out into the future?*** It should also answer the question: ***where will the money come from to pay those expenses?***

Creating a good retirement plan requires accurate information and the correct assumptions about what things are likely to cost in the future. This is the point where a great many people begin to get themselves into trouble.

A great deal of what passes for mainstream financial planning ignores the idea that you may be very happy with a lifestyle quite different and less expensive than the lifestyle you enjoyed while you were working. It also ignores the idea that your lifestyle will inevitably change as you get older. Considering those facts would not get you to where the financial services industry wants you to go.

Mainstream thinking from the financial services industry will start you off with a monthly expense budget in retirement that is essentially the same as—or a significant percentage of—what it was when you were working. Your expenses will then increase every year based upon a hypothetical rate of inflation and the unfounded belief that you will spend more every year as you get older.

Studies show that spending by retirees rarely keeps up with inflation and that spending actually peaks when people are in their early 80s. People tend to spend less each year after that.

Do not expect a salesperson connected with the financial services industry to have copies of these studies lying around.

The most common retirement planning and investment mistake is to believe in this phantom need for much greater income after you retire. The industry wants you to think that you will need more income so that you will invest more money with them *and* you will invest it more aggressively. The strategy is designed to maximize the industry's profit from every dollar invested.

A corollary is the mindset that your investments must make more money to satisfy this phantom need. The financial markets will not know that you are retired nor will they particularly care what kind of a return on your investments that you think you need.

Higher returns mean higher risks. Over time, real risks can mean real losses. ***It is really a terribly sick joke being played out against baby boomers by the financial industry.***

If you thought about it, you would plan your retirement around how much you will have to spend, rather than trying to make your portfolio earn what you think you will need. Retirees have far more control over the spending side of the retirement equation and can get immediate, predictable and direct results.

What do I tell people who tell me that they *need* to maximize the monthly check that their portfolio will generate? I tell them to change their lifestyle. If you cannot afford to retire, then do not. Keep working or get a new job. Start a small business. Downsize your home. Sell your season tickets. Do not visit your kids across the country as often; make them spend their money to visit you.

There are simple straightforward ways in which a competent financial professional can assist anyone to construct a portfolio that will provide these two things: 1) steady income and 2) longevity. If you invest your money appropriately you can get a reasonable return that is sustainable over the long-term. It is not that hard but neither is it that easy. Most people need to find the right advisor to help them; not one who hopes to maximize their own compensation from your account.

Sales presentations for financial products frequently throw out statistics and assumptions that are irrelevant at best and patently false at worst. They are intended to cause you to make very poor investment decisions. You should educate yourself so that you can understand which numbers are real, which numbers are assumed to be real and which are averages based upon what occurred in our parent's generation.

If you are going to invest for yourself, I would encourage you to take a college level course in financial planning and a separate course on investing. You should at the very least read a college level text that covers the various mathematical formulas that are commonly used—and understand why they are used.

It will help you to separate what you need to know from what salespeople are telling you that you need to know. Much of the common knowledge in the marketplace, and what passes for good math about retirement planning and retirement investing, can actually be harmful. That is the point.

If you are going to be an investor, then I believe that you should be able to crunch the numbers yourself. If you cannot, or even if you can, I recommend that you hire an investment advisor with number crunching ability. Either you know which numbers to crunch, how to crunch them and what your results mean or you should hire someone to advise you who does.

The retirement planning and investing process requires a realistic evaluation of how you might live after you retire. In our parents' generation, mom and pop stayed together until they died. A high percentage of baby boomers will be single when they retire.

If a couple in their 50s is separating, splitting the retirement accounts between them is likely to leave both with less than they need to retire separately. That is why old statistics, especially those for large groups of retirees are becoming less and less relevant.

If you have invested at all, you should know that past performance is not an indicator of future events. The mainstream retirement planning and investing process relies upon past performance on every level. You will hear about the past performance of the financial markets; you will hear about the past performance of specific investments and specific investment advisors. None of it may be relevant to you in any way.

The financial services industry will help you calculate your post-retirement needs and will convince you that you will need a lot more money to retire than you have. To have enough by the industry's standards, most people will need to buy riskier investments. Selling riskier investments is more profitable for the financial services industry than selling less risky investments.

To crank up the fear a notch or two, and perhaps to scare you into investing your money emotionally, the industry would have you ask the question: *will you run out of money before you die?* This is certainly a legitimate question. The answer is up to you.

If your investments, together with your other sources of income, pay out enough in dividends and interest every year, to pay your bills you should be fine. Once you begin to invade your principal to pay your bills you are on your way to the day when you actually might run out of money.

I would think that if your income does not cover your expenses, you would cut your expenses before you would invade your principal. If you do not have enough principal saved up to reasonably generate what you need, then either additional income from other sources or a lifestyle change is in order. That attitude, of course, would leave the financial services industry with nothing to sell you.

The financial industry addresses retirement investing with a promise to ***make your money work harder***. Every firm will promise to get you higher returns on your investments so that you will have more money to spend every month.

From the retirees' perspective it is an easy sale. A salesperson who can promise a customer an 8% return is more likely to get the sale than a salesperson promising a 6% return.

Government regulators call this *chasing yield.* Many people who are transitioning from work to fixed income naturally gravitate to promises of higher returns on their investments.

The promise to make your money work harder comes with two catches—higher risks and actual losses. At some point the risks associated with higher yields become *speculative,* meaning that there is a *substantial risk* that you will lose some or all of your money.

Much of the conventional wisdom about post-retirement investing is based upon the idea that you will spend more in the future because the things that you normally buy will cost more. You should therefore invest for a greater return, just to keep up with inflation.

Investments that pay a higher return frequently also pay substantially higher commissions, so promoting the idea that *you can and should earn more* is always in the financial services industry's best interest.

Once you start telling yourself that you *need* to make your portfolio work harder to maintain your lifestyle you are more likely than not going to get yourself in trouble. The market does not care that you are retired or that you really need this money. Your money earns more when you take more risks.

If you are already retired or close to it, and you expect to draw money from your retirement account every month to pay your bills you are, in my mind, an ***income investor***.

Traditionally, many investment advisors created laddered bond portfolios for older clients seeking steady income. The portfolio would include bonds with different maturity dates, which would be rolled over as they matured. The staggered interest rate exposure helped to keep the overall income relatively stable.

Bonds are considered to be relatively safe investments because the vast majority of bonds do pay off at maturity. Bonds are rated for their risk of default with riskier bonds paying higher interest rates to attract investors.

When interest rates in the market increase, new bonds being issued will pay higher interest and the value of the existing bonds in a portfolio will go down. An income investor holding bonds for income may not care, as they will get their money back when each bond matures.

A portfolio holding bonds until maturity needs little annual maintenance. Advisors who constructed these portfolios charged a markup or spread on the purchase of every bond but often charged a reduced annual account maintenance fee.

Since the credit market crash in 2008, the US Government, as well as other governments around the world, have kept interest rates artificially low. People who need income do not wish to keep their money in a savings account at a bank, which pays very little.

Savings accounts are insured by the US government and are considered to be safe. US Government bonds and some US Government agency bonds are also considered to be safe investments. All other investments have some degree of risk—the risk that you will not get some or all of your money back.

There are usually a variety of investments that can yield steady annual returns of 4% (with less risk) to 8% (with more risk) in almost any market environment. Some are bonds or other debt instruments. Some are dividend-paying shares.

Some are securities constructed to satisfy the financing needs of specific industries, such as real estate or oil and gas companies, that pass-through rents or royalties directly to investors. These securities all trade on the major exchanges and many are followed by professional research analysts.

Several chapters of this book are devoted to private real estate and oil and gas investments that mimic these public investments. Both may offer steady distributions to investors. Retirees for whom the public real estate or oil and gas investments might be suitable are too often steered to the private investments, which have a speculator's risk. The reason: much higher commissions are paid to the financial professionals who sell private investments.

Some financial advisors purchase bond funds for income investors. Bond funds are not the same as individual bonds. The portfolio held by a bond fund is susceptible to the same decline in value as interest rates rise but there is no maturity date for your shares in the fund. If interest rates go up your bond fund will be worth less and you can only sell your shares at the market price.

Bond funds may also buy junk bonds, foreign bonds, mortgage bonds, private debt or derivatives which may not continue to pay interest or which may not pay off at maturity. We saw all of these in bond funds that collapsed after the 2008 sell-off. You would be amazed how many stockbrokers and investment advisors never look at the actual portfolios of the bond funds that they are selling to their customers.

Before you purchase a *high-yield* bond fund you should know that they achieve that higher yield by taking greater risks. There is a reason that they call junk bonds "junk bonds." They default with significantly greater frequency than bonds that are rated as investment grade. High-yield bond funds are susceptible to both interest rate risk and the risk of default for some of their portfolio.

I always consider it a red flag if an advisor uses bond funds or bond ETFs instead of individual bonds or some other interest or dividend paying securities to create a portfolio for income investors. To me it is an indication that the advisor is unable to select individual bonds or is too lazy to take the time to do so.

The low interest rate environment that we have experienced since 2009 has caused many advisors to shift to other securities and instruments that make regular payments to investors. If you are an income investor, then the question to address during the core discussion that you have with any prospective investment advisor about generating income for your account is: ***individual bonds, bond funds or something else (and why)?***

It takes more skill and know-how for an advisor to construct an appropriate bond ladder than it does to select a bond fund. It takes more skill and know-how than either to research, evaluate and purchase other interest or dividend paying securities for an income portfolio.

If you are going to hire an investment advisor to help you invest for your retirement, my advice is to hire someone who is smart, experienced and aware.

This is 180° from the advice that the financial services industry would give to you. The new sales pitch from the industry suggests that retirement planning and retirement investing can be reduced to a few simple algorithms.

The industry will now tell you that there is no need for a financial planner, stockbroker, investment advisor or any intelligent human being to help you through the process—it is all automated.

Let me walk you through it.

CHAPTER II

Retirement Plans from Vending Machines

How much do you need to retire? At the very heart of the problem is the mindset that the financial services industry wants you to adopt. If you listen to the advertising and the so-called experts, the financial services industry will constantly remind you that every retiree should invest so that they can at least *maintain their pre-retirement lifestyle.*

While that may sound rational, it is not really a proper way in which to deal with the cold hard facts of retirement planning and investing.

Your post-retirement lifestyle is likely to be very different than your lifestyle during the years that you were working. Most people spend less every year that they are retired than they did when they were working. Many people spend less, year to year, as they get older.

Right there, the financial services industry will tell you that I am wrong; that people should expect to spend much more every year after they retire than they did while they were working. The entire retirement planning and investment industry is based upon this single idea, that it will take a lot more money to maintain your pre-retirement lifestyle after you retire. Not so.

Retirement itself is a lifestyle change. What you will spend every month after you retire will depend on you. If you have paid-off your mortgage, your monthly budget will be less. If you are planning to move to a smaller residence or another city, your monthly budget will certainly be different.

If you start your retirement planning with the idea that you will spend only what you can afford to spend on your lifestyle rather than insisting that your current lifestyle must be maintained, you will approach the subject with a much more rational perspective.

If you are like a lot of people, you will not have saved enough by the time you retire. We all know that tens of millions of baby boomers have no retirement savings at all. If you do have $500,000 to $1 million saved up, your natural instinct should be to protect your funds. Once you stop working, it may be difficult, if not impossible, to add to your account or replenish losses.

The financial services industry would prefer that you take some risk with your money. As I have already pointed out, riskier investments pay the industry more.

One of the most common, yet dangerous, financial tools available is the ***retirement expense calculator***. Even government agencies and respected consumer groups will provide them on their websites. These calculators can cause real headaches because they always direct investors to take on riskier investments.

A retirement calculator attempts to answer the question: *what will it cost in the future (after you are retired) to maintain your pre-retirement lifestyle?*

The answer that you will get from most retirement calculators is likely to be incorrect by a wide margin. Many financial planners and other financial professionals use the same or similar methodology and may also compute an answer that will not be anything close to what you will actually spend.

Retirement calculators will automatically factor in a minimum cost increase every year for inflation. The calculator is preset to increase your expenses every year. If you live into your 90s the calculator will tell you that you will be spending a small fortune on yourself every year.

Naturally, your portfolio will need to generate more and more money every year to keep up. The purpose of a retirement calculator is to get you used to the idea that you need to aggressively grow your portfolio until you die. People have been trained to accept the idea that they must take on more risk with their retirement funds.

Retirement calculators replicate some of the mainstream thinking about retirement planning and retirement investing. Unfortunately, the mainstream thinking about retirement planning and investing actually makes little or no common sense. More to the point, it makes sense only from the standpoint of the financial services industry.

Retirement calculators and much of what passes for professional financial planning are designed to skew the results to make retirees become more aggressive investors than they might need to be. This increases commissions, fees and overall profits to the financial services industry.

Retirement calculators multiply and divide but they do not think or reason. They do not know what is going on in your life or in the markets. They look at past performance and past performance only.

As with any statistical analysis, if you start with foolish assumptions or bad data, the end product is not likely to be very good. Retirement calculators rely on a series of foolish assumptions, which skews their results.

Assumption Number One: Your baseline income need is a percentage of your last year's earnings. Many retirement calculators start with the idea that one year after you retire, you will need 70% or 80% of your last working year's income to pay your bills. This is someone's idea of "average." Many people spend a lot less.

Every other calculation that the retirement calculator will do is based upon this baseline number: how much you will spend in the first year after you retire. So why plug in an average number instead of starting with your actual expense budget?

Some people will stay in their current home or community until they die; others will move to the Sunbelt, abroad or nearer to their grandchildren. Others may opt for an RV lifestyle. That is why I like the idea of using a certified financial planner; someone who plugs *your numbers* into the calculations, not *averages* and not the calculator's pre-programmed idea of how retirees live or will spend their money.

Assumption Number Two: Your expenses will continue to go up indefinitely. Inflation can be a thorny problem to anyone who is trying to live on a fixed income for a long time. One of the reasons that these retirement calculators always see growth in your expenses is that most automatically factor in a 3% or more annual rate of inflation.

Virtually all retirement planning starts with the idea that everything you buy today will cost more in the future. If you want to maintain your pre-retirement lifestyle and to be able to buy the same things every month in twenty years that you are buying today, you will need more money, every year, in order to be able to do so.

I do not want to minimize the effects of inflation on retirees, but overall inflation has been less than 3% annually for the last fifteen years. I do not want to suggest that I can predict the future, but simply assuming 3% growth in all expenses for every retiree is inaccurate and inappropriate.

A significant portion of many retirees' monthly expenses are fixed and few expenses increase at a rate of 3% per year in a straight line. Calculations that factor in a fixed 3% or more annual growth in all expenses due to inflation are the starting point for a result that is guaranteed to tell you: *if you want to maintain your lifestyle, then you will have to make your money work harder.*

How much you will actually need to spend every month after you retire is a very personal and individual calculation. Good financial planners will focus on *you* and how and where *you* will live after *you retire* and *what your real budget is likely to be* before they begin the process of determining which investments are the best for you.

Assumption Number Three: Your retirement lifestyle will be static. A retirement calculator assumes that you will be purchasing the same products and services in twenty years that you are purchasing today. Lifestyles change as people get older. This was true from our 20s to our 40s; our 40s to our 60s and it will continue to be true as we approach 80 years of age and beyond.

As retirees get older, they report less travel and entertainment-related expenses and frequently higher medical costs. Statistically at least, most people slow down and spend less money when they get older, not more.

If you are close to retirement age now, and you expect to live to be 85 years of age or older, you should plan for it. Do not assume that the monthly purchases that you will be making then will necessarily be that same ones that you are making today. You should take a realistic look at where you expect to live and what you expect to be doing.

A financial plan prepared by a retirement calculator will not consider that you might need long-term care or what it might cost. You would be foolish to prepare a financial plan by just multiplying your expenses by a hypothetical rate of inflation rather than looking at how you might actually be living and what it might actually cost. Unfortunately, millions of people do.

Assumption Number Four: You will really need much more money if you live considerably longer. If you prepare your financial plan with a retirement calculator, on the right side or bottom right side of the expense chart will be the amount of money the calculator says that you will expect to spend in the year of your 100th or 110th birthday. This number is likely to be more money than you ever earned in any ten years of your life.

You get to this number by starting with the assumption you will need 70% or more of your last year's income when you retire and that inflation will increase your costs by 3% or more per year. It is unlikely that you will need to spend this much in any year, especially if you are that old. This is a warning that these calculators are putting out numbers that make no sense.

An investment portfolio that would be attempting to get to this level in 30-35 years without reinvesting dividends (which you will be spending) will likely need to take some higher risks. Over 30-35 years, the more risks that you take, the more likely that some of those risks will come back to bite you.

If you are not going to actually need this much money when you are that old, why are you taking the extra risks necessary to obtain this return? Perhaps it is because higher risk investments frequently pay higher commissions and fees to the people who sell them.

Assumption Number Five: Your expenses will determine how much you will draw from your account every year. If you start with the idea that you will need to draw as much as possible from your retirement account every month, you are looking for trouble. If you are going to start pressing your portfolio to generate higher returns, you are going to take higher risks and you are likely to sustain losses.

Many experts suggest that you should draw out no more than 4% of your portfolio's value in any one year. The retirement calculator is intended to show you in black and white that if your portfolio needs to earn 4% each year to pay your bills, then you will need to earn another 3% to adjust the portfolio for inflation. ***If you believe this to be true then you are on the precipice of a very slippery slope.***

A better idea would be to set up your portfolio to earn a certain amount of dividends and interest every year and to draw out a little less than you earn. If you are willing to live with that, then, statistically, you can probably do just fine.

The retirement calculator will inevitably demonstrate that you have a problem—not enough income growth to keep up with inflation. It will tell you that you will need more money every year in order to maintain your lifestyle after you retire.

It will steer you to the financial services industry, which always has ways to make your money work harder so that you can earn more. That is why retirement calculators exist. People who use retirement calculators are invariably steered into investments that purport to yield more.

Over the years I have heard people say that for the long-term the stock market appreciates by an average of 10% per year, usually including reinvested dividends. There is apparently no relevant data that supports that statistic.

I have never seen an academic study that has reached that conclusion and there is no reason whatsoever to believe that the

"10% average annual appreciation" for the stock market is anything more than market lore. Even if true, it would be largely irrelevant.

If you do believe that the stock market could appreciate by an average of 10% every year, then you must at least concede that it might rise or fall by more or less than that average amount in any given year. If your $1 million dollar stock portfolio might decline in value by 10% or more for a year or two, you might find yourself with $750,000 or less in no time at all.

Investment risk is quite real and can be quite life changing if you lose. It might be even more life changing if you started with $500,000 and "market action" reduced it to $325,000.

There are studies that do validate the idea that if your portfolio does sustain losses in consecutive years, especially in the early years after you have begun to draw from it, it is likely that your portfolio will run dry in 25 years or less.

If your portfolio is invested in stocks and you expect to pay you bills from the average appreciation of the market, then taking fixed distributions, adjusted for inflation, from your account over the long-term will likely drain your portfolio.

You will inevitably run into some down markets and sustain some losses. If you do live into your 90s or have extraordinary bills for your care, running out of money can become a reality.

I do not have to tell you that being old and broke is not a good combination.

Of course none of this makes any difference if you do not have a reasonable retirement account when you retire. The financial services industry has a lot invested in getting baby boomers who do to deposit their funds.

It has already set its eyes on millennials who collectively will bring more money to the market.

CHAPTER III

The Mathematics of Investing

The most basic mathematics of retirement planning and investing suggest that one way to create a retirement fund is to start an account when you are young, add to it every year and invest for the long-term. If you continue to add to the account into your 50s and 60s and keep reinvesting the interest and dividends, a retirement account worth a million dollars or more is not only possible, but achievable.

This is a "Rule of 72" calculation, which is one of the very first calculations that you should make regarding retirement investment planning. The Rule of 72 tells you how long it will take for your money to double if your rate of return is fixed and you compound the interest.

At an annual rate of 6%, for example, whatever you put away today will double in just about 12 years. I intend to use 6% as a base rate for income-producing investments throughout. It is obtainable with a suitable mix of dividend and income producing securities.

By base rate, I mean to judge other investments against this annual rate of return. I specifically will look at how much additional risk investors will take to get a potentially better return.

You can fill a portfolio with bonds that are safer than any stocks that you can buy. People invest in stocks seeking a better return than a portfolio of bonds. The risk is that you might end up with substantially less. Bonds will usually pay off at par on a fixed maturity date. A stock may never again be worth as much as you pay for it.

The easiest way for you to understand the mathematics of risk is to answer the question: *how much of the money that you are investing are you prepared to lose*? Not how much do you think you might lose, but how much are you actually prepared to lose and not lose sleep over?

If you are already retired and you have a million dollars invested in a portfolio of stocks and the market declines by 25 or 30% and stays down for a while, would you be uncomfortable? Would you still have enough left to pay your bills for as long as you live?

If you deal with a financial adviser, then *how much might I lose* is a question that is appropriate to any discussion about any investment or strategy. You should also ask if the advisor has a strategy to limit the losses to any specific level.

Some retirees are advised to keep their funds in the stock market after they retire. Advisors seeing retirements that they believe will likely last 25 or 30 years or more seemingly believe that long-term portfolio growth necessarily overrides any prudence regarding long-term exposure to market risks.

The thing about market risks is that over the long term they frequently turn into market losses.

If you are invested in a stock portfolio for the long term, it will likely be managed according to the principles of asset allocation specifically to help reduce some of that risk. Asset allocation is based upon the historical, long-term cyclical movements of the debt and equity markets. It is a mainstream tool for long-term portfolio construction and management.

We believe that asset allocation works to reduce portfolio risk because of observations that were made about the supply and demand for debt instruments and the effect of interest rates on corporate profits. Simply, when interest rates are high, investors will want to invest in debt, looking to lock in high returns.

At that same time in the market cycle, companies seeking capital will often respond by selling equities rather than drain their cash flow. When interest rates are low, companies want to borrow. Low borrowing costs can increase earnings-per-share and share prices with them.

Asset allocation suggests that investors should hold some percentage of their portfolios in stocks, some percentage in bonds and some amount of cash. The object is to maintain this same allocation percentage into the future as market conditions change.

Existing bonds will decrease in value when interest rates rise. When they are worth less, a greater percentage of the same portfolio will be allocated to equities, because equities will be worth more relative to the bonds. Asset allocation will direct you to sell off some of the "excess" stocks and purchase more bonds at the greater yield.

How much you might make if the market rises is always offset by how much you might lose if prices fall. Asset allocation reduces portfolio risks—specifically the risks of the ebb and flow of market cycles.

The net result of an asset allocation strategy is that you should not lose too much, but neither will you see the markets' most robust gains. People invest in the stock market specifically to obtain those higher returns.

Diversification is a mathematical model based upon the idea that certain types of companies do better or worse under different economic conditions. Diversification seeks to strike a balance where some positions in the portfolio will do well when others do poorly as economic conditions change. At the same time, it seeks to disperse these economic risks among a large number of companies.

To work correctly, diversification requires an assessment of the *correlation* (positive or negative) of the various investments that you will actually purchase in the portfolio. You may make an investment in an oil company, for example, whose share price may decline as oil prices decline. The stock of that company might have a negative correlation with an airline, which might be expected to see profits rise with cheaper fuel costs.

Understand that while an oil company and an airline might have an opposite or negative correlation to an oil price decline, the shares of both might suffer at a time when unemployment is high because retail customers become scarcer.

Companies will correlate differently to different economic conditions. The math can be somewhat complex. It has been made more difficult by globalization. Many companies which sell or source products in many global markets are subject to risks that are difficult to identify and harder to quantify.

From here the math gets even more complex. Predicting which segments of the market will do better than others under current or anticipated market conditions requires a tremendous amount of data.

While I understand fundamental securities analysis and a little about technical analysis, I still hire a professional advisor to select specific investments for me. It takes time and effort to do it right.

Throughout this book I will highlight instances where advisors do it wrong. In this instance, the best example that I can offer of how **not** to construct a portfolio is the new automated investment tool called the ***automatic asset allocator and re-***

balancer. Generically, they are called ***robo-investment advisors or robo-advisors***.

Robo-advisors are targeted at millennials. Millennials still have a long way until they retire and they seem just as comfortable with an automated system as with a live financial advisor because they do not understand the difference. If they took the time to learn about investing, they would not go near these programs.

The programs dispense no real advice. They are constructed for convenience, not how well they might actually construct an investment portfolio. They are premised on the idea that the markets will do in the next 30 years what it did 30-50 years ago. Given how fast and how profoundly the financial markets have changed just in the last 15 years, everything that robo-advisor advertising is telling you—about how well these programs will help you to prepare for the distant future—is not likely to come true.

The sales pitch for a robo-advisor will assure you that it will help you construct a long-term investment portfolio while dealing with market risks. It will promise to use the principles of asset allocation and rebalancing to smooth out the market cycles. No need to concern yourself with the math, the sales pitch will tell you, the automated program will do it all for you.

Robo-advisor ads also promise that you will have no need for a human advisor. At least one program touts that it is free of human error. All of what has been considered good financial advice for the last generation is out the window.

When I began in the securities industry, the first rule of the business was *"know your customer."* Registered representatives built long-term relationships with their clients. There is no place for that rule or that way of thinking with a robo-advisor. It is never going to get to know you. The industry has apparently decided that millenials are not worth getting to know.

Using a robo-advisor is less expensive than using a live broker. Customers pay less to use a robo-advisor because they get much less. I do not believe that any customer actually gets a portfolio that makes sense from any of these programs.

The process usually begins with an on-screen questionnaire. A few simple questions and the program will help you set up a suitable investment portfolio. It is going to help you determine your risk tolerance and then help you select a portfolio suitable to your age and risk tolerance.

Portfolio selection presumes that either the customers know what they are doing or the program can steer them to an appropriate choice. There is no indication whatsoever that any of these programs can actually do so.

Customers, by thinking that a computer program can replace a good advisor, demonstrate that they do not know what they are doing, either.

Robo-advisors give lip service to asset allocation, applying this principle only on the most superficial level. They do not do the hard work. These models are unlikely, for example, to suggest that a large portion of your portfolio ever be held in cash, even in times of market transition or uncertainty.

If you ask the program, *"Which sector ETFs should I buy under current market conditions?"*, most of the programs will have no answer. That question and ones like it are why people pay live human beings to advise them about investments.

The program also claims that it will help you manage the portfolio for the next 30 years or more. As the markets move and the original allocation becomes out-of-balance, the program will automatically alert you to buy and sell positions in order to rebalance the portfolio to the original allocation. This is fine as far as it goes, but most of these programs cannot really go much further.

The program also assumes that a lot of what has existed previously in the markets will continue into the future. At its core the program is looking to the past performance of the market. It is investment advice that basically says: *this is how the markets have acted in the past, we advise you to invest as if everything will continue as before.*

What is remarkable to me is that millennials, who see every other market rapidly evolving, do not catch on.

If you have any doubt that these robo-advisor programs are less than worthless, consider some of the patently foolish assumptions upon which the robo-advisor industry rests its foundation.

Assumption Number One: It is all about your age. One of the few personal questions that an asset allocator will ask is your age. If you are thirty, the program will assume that you can afford to take more risk than a person who is sixty. The reasoning is that 1) you will want to get a jump to get your account going early and 2) if you make a mistake and take some losses, you still have a lot of years to catch up. Using this logic, the program should always buy fewer stocks for investors who are older or who want to be more conservative.

The portfolios that the computer may serve up for you are based upon the historic relationship between stocks and bonds. Actual market conditions computed for today are not used.

The data that the program uses to select portfolios is the past performance of the markets. I should not have to tell you that past performance is an unreliable indicator of future results.

Investing based upon your age assumes that your age and the markets are somehow related. What you should or should not buy today is dependent upon the market, not upon your age. If you start down this path, what you will have bought or sold over the years that you stay with the program will have had nothing to do with what might have been a good investment at any time.

Assumption Number Two: Today is a good day to invest in either stocks or bonds. Let us say that the program suggests that you create a portfolio today that is 35% bond funds or bond ETFs; 60% stock funds or ETFs and 5% cash. If you begin investing this year when the market averages are making new highs, it is reasonable to expect that next year or the year after, the market might correct. It is very possible that five years down the road, 60% of your portfolio will be worth less than it is today.

After seven years of forced low interest rates, is this a good time to put 35% of your money into bond funds? Savvy investors know that bond funds do not do well when interest rates rise. Does the computer program know this and will it adjust for it or just take the losses? If we have successive rate hikes over the next few years or longer, will the program take the losses every time?

Assumption Number Three: Investing can be done in a vacuum. The computer program does not get a live news feed and would not know if Germany had invaded Poland, so events leading up to any crisis that might affect the markets would necessarily be ignored. The program does not concern itself with commodity prices, currency rates or international politics. Just past performance.

To my mind, using a robo-investment advisor to construct and manage your long-term portfolio is the same as making all of your investment decisions from inside a small closet, with the door closed and the lights off.

Assumption Number Four: The markets will be static for the next 30 years. The noted theorists, upon whose works Modern Portfolio Theory, asset allocation and diversification are based, were examining and extrapolating data from the markets prior to 1990. The financial markets themselves are vastly different today than they were at that time. It is not just the speed or the technology. The markets are global, there are a lot more participants and there is a lot more money in play. How the markets will evolve and operate in the next 25 years is anyone's guess.

There should be no real expectation that the financial markets will continue to operate or act as they have in the past. These programs may someday catch up. But they just as well may not.

The sales pitch for these robo-advisors suggests that millennials can put away money each year and invest it with the help of the software. There is no indication that the software will ever suggest that they cash out completely, so many customers are likely to stay with the program until the market crashes. Perhaps then, they will wise up.

Assumption Number Five: It is all about the math. I believe that investing is very much about mathematics. The numbers that you look at should be the relevant numbers, analyzed in the right way. But it is not only about the numbers.

The robo-advisor never gets past a limited set of gross market data. A robo-advisor never actually looks at any company's balance sheet. I would want to know about products in the pipeline, potential competitors and what the new CEO is thinking about. A robo-advisor is never interested in the things that most other investors would want to know.

Robo-advisor advocates would counter that robo-advisors use sophisticated algorithms to analyze the data and to make appropriate recommendations. Sophisticated algorithms do exist and are used by some market traders. However sophisticated the software may be, the software is not picking up the bulk of the relevant information it would need. A robo-advisor cannot make a sophisticated investment recommendation. It just follows a script: if A, then B.

Assumption Number Six: Human beings are not necessary. To correctly construct a long-term investment portfolio requires knowledge of the mathematics of investing and also of the economics of the marketplace. Understanding the interrelationship between market sectors, interest rates, commodity prices, currency rates and international politics can be essential to a portfolio manager's success. This would seem to be especially true as markets expand and globalize.

I firmly believe that you should utilize the services or a professional financial advisor. I believe that the person from whom you seek financial advice before you retire is the key person who will be responsible for determining exactly how much money you will have to spend between the time that you retire and the time that you die.

Using a robo-advisor will inevitably lead to portfolio losses every time the stock market goes down or the interest rates go up. Severe market downturns can be scary. Investors are prone to panic. When your account value is dropping, you are going to want someone to call. The robo-advisor will offer neither solace nor advice. For that you have to pay a little more and get a flesh and blood financial advisor.

But first, you must avoid those advisors who are out and out thieves. And they are everywhere.

CHAPTER IV
Boiler Rooms

I was impressed when I first read *The Wolf of Wall Street.* I have never met Jordan Belfort. From the book, he seems quite affable.

I did represent several customers of Mr. Belfort's firm, Stratton Oakmont, who had been defrauded by Mr. Belfort's pump and dump schemes. Stratton Oakmont was not the first pump and dump operator that I had seen nor was it the most sophisticated. It was certainly not the last.

The real story of *The Wolf of Wall Street* is how much fun Mr. Belfort had with the money that he stole from his customers. Americans love scoundrels and Mr. Belfort was certainly that.

Stratton Oakmont did represent a classic example of a boiler-room based pump and dump scheme for its time. There are always similar schemes being run by someone. I thought that I would explain how Stratton Oakmont ran their scam. The next time someone tells you about *the greatest investment opportunity of all time,* maybe you will not get sucked in.

The key to any stock manipulation is getting a lot of stock cheap, before you start to pump up the price. Stratton Oakmont, for example, might acquire two million shares of the company for $.05 per share before the brokers manned the phones. In some cases, they pumped the price up to $10 or $20 per share or more before they sold out. You can see why the potential for profit is enormous.

Stratton Oakmont was responsible for the IPO of the companies whose stock was being manipulated. It could literally offer cheap, pre-IPO stock to its friends. The friends would hold their shares until the brokers had pushed the price much higher. Then they sold out.

By being the underwriter for the IPO, Stratton knew who owned virtually every share of stock of the company that they were working. Unlike normal stocks whose price is set by buyers and sellers acting freely in the market, for many of these stocks the only market was at Stratton Oakmont. The only price at which anyone could buy these stocks was for more than they cost yesterday.

The Stratton Oakmont brokers would generate a considerable amount of excitement about a company as the stock price ran up. When they had a considerable number of people interested in buying the stock at a high price, the insiders dumped the cheap stock that they were holding and moved on to the next company.

Stratton bought lists of telephone numbers for doctors and business owners. A Stratton Oakmont broker would call you on the phone, introduce himself or herself and tell you about the enormous investment opportunity that you would be foolish to pass up.

They would ask you up front if you had $10,000 or more to invest. The Stratton Oakmont brokers would work from a script that would have them repeat all of the good things about the company whose stock they were selling.

The *boiler-room* aspect of Stratton Oakmont's operation analogizes to the *high pressure* that the brokers used in order to convince people to send in their checks.

- **The price of the stock is about to go up.**
- **A big institutional buyer has been sniffing around.**
- **Act fast. I only have 10,000 shares left.**
- **The company is going to make a big announcement.**
- **Don't get left behind. Quick. Quick. Quick.**

The *high pressure* is designed to create a sense of *urgency* to make the potential customer act without delay and without thinking. A Stratton Oakmont broker might say: *You write out the check and leave it an envelope with your receptionist. I will have Fedex pick it up.*

A personal favorite: *What do you mean you need to ask your wife before you can send me $50,000?Are you the decision maker in your own home, sir, or not?*

If a prospective customer was too polite (meaning they did not hang up immediately) then the pitch got more frequent and more urgent. If you did not send a check yesterday or the day before, and even if you had specifically declined to send a check, they would keep calling. A lot of people did not send their check until the fifth telephone call or beyond.

Stratton brokers could be relentless and for good reason. If they called you last month when the stock was $2 per share and last week when the stock was $6 per share and you said no both times, you might relent now that it is $8 per share because the broker had told you it was going to $16 per share on both of the first two calls. Still not convinced?

If you did not buy stock A which ran up to $20 per share as predicted and stock B which ran up to $25 per share, how reluctant will you be when the broker calls you with stock C at $2 per share and tells you that this will outshine the other two. It is easy for the broker to set up this scenario when the broker knows the price of all the stocks is being manipulated.

At its core, the sales pitch from the Stratton broker says: *send me your money and I will make you money. You do not have to do anything. I have special knowledge and even though I do not know you, I am calling you up at random so that I can share my knowledge with you and you will profit from it. All you have to do to win is send me your money. So pardon me if I get frustrated because you do not know a gift when you see one.*

People actually believed that it was their good fortune that a perfect stranger had sought them out and was willing to help them earn a hefty profit. That seeming incongruity is what Stratton Oakmont and similar illicit boiler-room operators exploited.

High-pressure sales pitches never go out of style among those people who want to *use their words to steal other people's money*. They do not go out of style because they work. If you are not smart enough to say *no thank you* within the first fifteen seconds of a call from a broker offering you an unsolicited stock tip, then you are leaving the door open to being scammed.

Everyone in the boiler room, the brokers and managers and certainly Mr. Belfort and his partners, knew that every person who sent a check to them would never see their money again. Even if they had not lost all of their money in the trading scam, Stratton Oakmont actually refused to send people their own money back, even if they still had some left.

Stratton Oakmont pumped up the price of the shares of about twenty different companies. When it was over, many hundreds of millions of dollars from thousands of unknowing investors were in the pockets of Mr. Belfort and his cohorts. From all accounts, they enjoyed spending it.

Stratton Oakmont was not the first boiler room, nor the last. Old-timers like me can remember Blinder Robinson in the 1980s and First Jersey Securities before them. The owner of the latter firm starred in his own TV commercials, stepping out of a helicopter, touting his desire to fund *America's emerging growth companies*. The owners of those boiler rooms made a lot of money as well.

There is also a detailed record of organized crime being linked to boiler rooms and stock manipulations going back to at least the 1970s and becoming more prevalent into the 1990s. Stock manipulation is a remarkably easy way to make a lot of money—illegally.

As an attorney, I have always learned from watching how other attorneys handle various situations. At the time, Stratton Oakmont had some of the best legal representation available. These lawyers devised some unique strategies. They were able to keep the doors open at Stratton and the scam going long after the regulators knew what was going on.

In 1994, the Internet was not yet as developed as we know it today and new channels for financial news were still evolving. Commercial services like CompuServe and Prodigy provided *bulletin boards* where investors could post their thoughts about various stocks and investments.

An investor posted a comment on Prodigy stating that Stratton Oakmont was committing securities fraud. Stratton Oakmont responded by suing Prodigy claiming that Prodigy had defamed Stratton Oakmont by accepting the post. Stratton Oakmont won.

More importantly, in any defamation action the best defense is to assert that the offending statement is not defamatory because it is true. Because they sued Prodigy, Stratton Oakmont was able to steer the conversation away from *"did they really commit securities fraud"* and instead to whether or not Prodigy, the bulletin board, should be responsible for allowing a post containing negative sentiments about anyone.

The case was defended by excellent attorneys who specialized in the defense of defamation actions. If they had used securities lawyers to defend the case, more likely than not the fraud could have been proved.

Like I said, Stratton Oakmont won in court against Prodigy. It was a skillful legal maneuver and Stratton Oakmont demonstrated to everyone that they would not just admit to their crimes. Stratton Oakmont initially won against the regulators as well.

There were as many as a dozen regulatory actions against Stratton Oakmont and its principals over a period of many years before the SEC was able to finally close them down. During those years, after securities regulators knew how Stratton was operating, Stratton continued to fight the regulators, remained open and continued to steal tens of millions of dollars from thousands of people.

So how much money did Stratton Oakmont actually steal? The best estimates indicate that they stole between $5-$10 million dollars on each of the more than twenty stocks they manipulated. That would mean that Mr. Belfort and his partners stole somewhere between $100 and $200 million dollars.

The individual brokers were willing participants in the scam and were well paid for getting on the telephone and convincing strangers to send in their money. If the boiler room had 100 brokers making 100 cold calls a day, they might reach 200,000 potential customers a month and perhaps signup 2000. Some reports estimated that Stratton Oakmont brokers made more than one million phone calls a month.

The individual brokers were also Mr. Belfort's biggest expense. In addition to a huge slice of the funds that they brought in, as detailed in the book, Mr. Belfort spent extravagant sums for bonuses, perks, parties and drugs to keep the brokers on the phones. All of this was paid for with the funds sent in by people who believed the lies that the brokers told about company after company.

Today it is far cheaper and easier to perpetrate a pump and dump scheme than ever before. The boiler rooms, which were at the center of these schemes twenty years ago, have been supplanted by new avenues of communications that have far greater reach and far less cost.

The Internet provides chat rooms and tip sheets and cable networks provide analysts, experts and pundits whose *words can cause the price of any stock to go up or down.* The average investor has no idea how to separate good advice from ridiculous chatter or to discern whose financial interests are being served by the information that they are receiving.

People believe what they want to believe and over the years a good rumor has caused a great many shares of a great many companies to change hands.

I currently get several stock-tip newsletters via email every week, each of which purports to have thousands of subscribers. Each of these newsletters effectively uses the Internet to put themselves and the stocks that they are touting in front of a great many more potential customers than a boiler room could, for a fraction of what a boiler room would cost. For the most part, these electronic newsletters are not regulated.

This is the *disclaimer* that comes with one of those electronic newsletters:

"The ***** Newsletter is an electronic publication committed to providing readers with useful information on publicly-traded companies. *The Newsletter sometimes contracts with third parties or publicly traded companies and receives compensation from them in the form of cash and sometimes restricted securities as payment for publishing information and opinion about the company and the trading market for their securities. Principals of the Newsletter may also purchase or sell securities of the companies in the open market from time to time."*

They are telling you that they have *cheap stock.* That in and of itself should make anyone who reads these newsletters very wary. This is not the same thing as a research analyst at a large firm who may take a position in a stock that they cover. This is *cheap stock,* the type of stock that stock manipulators own. *This disclaimer is a red flag. Walk away.*

What? I want you to read the legal *disclaimer* and pretend that it has meaning? Every item that you buy, including toasters, comes with a legal disclaimer and no one pays any attention at all.

The US federal securities laws are grounded on the idea that investors are entitled to full, fair and accurate disclosure of all of the material facts about any investment. That includes information about financial conflicts that might color investment advice.

Here is a disclosure that essentially says: *I am publishing a newsletter encouraging you to buy shares in these companies at the same time I am likely going to be selling the shares that I already own and acquired cheaply.*

You can see why investing $10,000 or $100,000 dollars in a company touted by a newsletter may be good for the newsletter publisher—but not for anyone else.

Today, one person could effectively run a pump and dump scam on the Internet from their kitchen table and steal many millions of dollars. If that person happens to be operating from another country or even if they are not, it is unlikely that any money that anyone sends to them will be recovered.

In the spring of 2014, the SEC shut down an opt-in financial newsletter called **AwesomePennyStocks.com.** The SEC alleged that it was run by a 24-year-old Canadian gentleman who manipulated dozens of stocks over a period of years using handheld smartphones. Unlike Mr. Belfort, he had neither rent nor salespeople to pay. Beginning before his 21st birthday and essentially working alone, this gentleman may have stolen hundreds of millions of dollars and perhaps much more.

Although the SEC is usually somewhat tight-lipped about these ongoing investigations, in the context of a divorce filing, it appears that his wife is telling stories about exotic cars, offshore companies and millions laundered here and there.

Each year, more and more people contact me and tell me that the company with which they dealt, and which they want me to sue for them, was *offshore*. As the financial markets globalize there will be more and more opportunities for people to invest in emerging markets and for people in other countries to invest here.

Ask yourself: *why am I taking the extra risk of dealing with an offshore company or making an investment in another country?* There is a higher risk that you will be scammed and very little that you will be able to do about it if you are.

If an investment sounds too good to be true, it probably is. If someone is *pressuring* you, even subtly, to make a substantial investment *quickly* for whatever reason, and it just does not feel right, walk away.

An observation: when I interview a married couple who lost money in a joint investment account, frequently it is the husband who was the primary actor of the two when it came to purchasing the offending investments. On more than one occasion, enough to warrant being included in this book, the wife gratuitously remarked how she was not certain that she had trusted the salesperson at the time. More than one used words like *sleazy* or *oily* or *unctuous*.

If you are making any investment, no matter how good it sounds, and your gut (or your spouse's gut) says *whoa,* then by all means, take your money and invest it somewhere that you will be more comfortable.

Missing out on a *terrific investment opportunity* is not as painful or disastrous to your financial health as flushing a lot of your money down the financial toilet.

There have always been scam artists in the financial markets who want to steal your money. Be smart—do not let them.

Retirees who spend a lot of time doing their own financial research on the Internet are especially susceptible to investment frauds because *they know just enough to get themselves into trouble.*

You are unlikely to realize that you have been caught up in a stock manipulation until it is over. If you have doubts, keep you money in your pocket.

Retirees purchase hundreds of billions of dollars of phony investments every year. Like the scripts used by the boiler rooms, many sound good. Some, like the boiler room stocks, will simply evaporate.

CHAPTER V

Private Notes and Ponzi Schemes

Two central themes of this book are as follows: Investments that offer higher than average yields typically have higher than average risks. At the same time, because these investments have higher risks, people who sell these investments receive a higher than average commission for doing so.

Companies that issue stocks and bonds that trade on an exchange or other organized public market are required to follow some basic rules regarding how they present their financial information and how and what they disclose to potential investors. With private companies, some of those basic rules are often ignored.

A promissory note is a form of debt that companies sometimes use, like loans, to raise money. The company issuing the notes promises to return the buyer's funds (principal) and to make fixed-interest payments to the buyer in exchange for borrowing the money. Promissory notes have set terms, or repayment periods, ranging from a few months to several years.

There is a large, private market for institutional debt, promissory notes and similar instruments issued by large companies and purchased by insurance companies, large pension plans and funds. The large companies and institutional investors will frequently negotiate and structure a transaction that suits the interests of both. There are a great many ways in which an investment transaction can be structured.

Individual investors rarely have the sophistication to do their own research on the company issuing the notes to determine whether the notes are a good deal. ***The fact that promissory notes are being sold to smaller individual investors is itself a red flag.***

Even legitimate promissory notes can involve high risks. Creditworthiness is the markets' determination of whether or not the company will pay the loan as the note dictates. The less creditworthy the company is, the less likely that you will be repaid.

One of the basic rules of the financial markets is that the most creditworthy borrowers pay the lowest rate of interest. Any creditworthy business that can borrow the same funds from a bank at prime plus 2% will not be offering to pay investors 12% or 15% or more in the private markets.

Retirees who are looking to increase their monthly income may be offered private notes that pay higher rates of interest. These notes are likely not from creditworthy borrowers. Your risk that the borrower will not pay you as promised is high. The risk that you will lose some or all of your money is high as well.

The higher the rate of interest that the company is willing to pay you in order to get your money, the greater the risk that you will not be paid as promised.

Many of these companies are legitimate businesses and many of the people behind them work hard making the businesses successful for themselves and for their investors. Not all.

Retirees and others who might buy these private notes might hear a sales pitch that might include:

- **Investors will receive a very high, *double digit amount of interest,***
- **Returns are *guaranteed,* or,**
- **The notes are *fully secured or fully collateralized.***

It all sounds good, but is any of it true?

The private securities markets are far less regulated and far less transparent than the public markets. Accurate financial information about the companies that are raising funds is at the core of the public markets. Financial information is much less available and far more questionable in the private markets.

A good rule: ***If you cannot get solid, audited, financial information about a company that wants you to loan it money, pass.***

Ask yourself: *how can the business underlying the investment generate that much cash flow to be able to pay investors 12% or 15% return on capital?*

The interest rate reflects the markets' opinion that the company cannot make the payments. To counter that, many high interest notes will come with a story or explanation of exactly how this company will earn enough to pay you back. The story is part of the sales pitch. It may not be true.

Ask yourself: *if sophisticated market professionals can get the same 12% or 15% or better return that is being offered to you, why did they pass?*

I have asked many people: *Were you at all suspicious when the salesperson told you that this note was fully secured and would still pay you 15%?*

In response I have gotten a great many blank stares from a great many otherwise intelligent people who heard *fully secured* and *15%* and handed over their retirement funds counting on those monthly checks.

I have come to the conclusion that if you handed over your money, you obviously were not suspicious enough.

On a good day an investor seeking a high return in the private securities markets will invest in a company that is a very bad credit risk. On a bad day, the same investor seeking the same high return might invest into a **Ponzi scheme.**

The difference between a high yield investment in the private securities market and an investment into a Ponzi scheme is often the honesty of the people who are running the company into which you are investing. Some people will take your money and really try to make their business work. The operator of a Ponzi scheme is a thief.

I cannot recall a Ponzi scheme run by someone who was trying to secure cancer treatments for their impoverished parents. When the forensic accountants add up the swag accumulated by most Ponzi scheme operators there are frequently yachts, expensive jewelry and lavish lifestyles—all paid for with the investors' money.

No one is surprised when the brokers who helped bring investors into the scheme are also found to have been well-compensated. I have witnessed a succession of less than honest operators who paid themselves high front-end fees and who lavished golf trips and big parties on the stockbrokers and others who would bring trusting investors to their door.

People frequently think of Bernie Madoff when the subject of Ponzi schemes comes up. For years, Mr. Madoff claimed to provide above average returns to his investors, ostensibly from his proprietary trading and portfolio management. There were not actually any trading profits; indeed, there were not actually many trades.

Payments that Mr. Madoff made to his investors were either their own money being returned that he called *profits* or the funds Mr. Madoff collected from new investors. New investors begged him to manage their money because he was apparently doing so well. The operation of a Ponzi scheme is all about appearances.

Ponzi schemes are actually a lot more common than you might think and are often offered to retirees and other investors who are seeking higher income. The fact that there are so many dishonest operators in the private securities markets is enough of a reason for many people who might want to invest there to stay away.

Over the years I witnessed a local real estate developer (whom everyone loved for his charity work in the community) borrow money to fund his developments by selling promissory notes secured by first trust deeds on real estate. After a while it was discovered that he had sold notes secured by the first position on the same property to dozens of different people. The developer just pocketed the difference.

I have seen real life schemes similar to *The Producers*, where nonexistent films and Broadway stage productions were funded. I have seen millions of dollars raised for nonexistent new drugs and nonexistent gold mines and oil wells. I have seen investors shocked when the young entrepreneur who was building a new business took their money and moved away.

A more typical Ponzi scheme takes some of the investors' money and gives it back to them, every month, seemingly paying a high dividend. People hear about this great investment or some broker tells them about it and the Ponzi scheme suddenly has millions and millions of dollars.

The promise of consistent high income is common to all Ponzi schemes. Ponzi schemes tend to collapse very quickly when people start to ask for their money back and it is not there.

High yield is the bait that snares investors and makes Ponzi schemes profitable for the thieves that operate them. Each scheme always comes with a great story about how the company can earn enough money to pay out 12% or 15% or more to investors and still make a profit.

In one recent case a real estate company called **DBSI** was issuing bonds at 16% claiming that the rising real estate market would cover the payments. The scam went on for years with people ultimately investing more than $800 million.

When the scheme finally collapsed, which they always do, about $80 million was missing. The money had been funneled into the pockets of the people who had started and operated the company.

DBSI bonds and other DBSI securities were sold by a number of large stockbrokerage firms that ***should have known better.*** All logic suggests that a company that was dealing with hundreds of millions of dollars of investors' money would have an annual audit so that everyone would be certain that the company, at least financially, was on the up and up.

Auditors do not guarantee that a financial crime is not being committed. They do attempt to ascertain whether or not the company is spending according to its obligations. Without an auditor looking over their shoulder, the managers at DBSI could conceal their theft.

I single out DBSI because it did present an unaudited balance sheet to prospective investors. The financial information was presented in such a way that it made the company look solvent and successful.

Anyone who had taken the time to reorganize the information that the company presented on its financial statements into standard form would have seen that the company was insolvent as early as 2004.

Investors who purchased DBSI bonds in 2005 or later were given false information about DBSI at the time that they invested. Brokers who sold these bonds did not disclose the true facts about the company. Few had ever looked at the balance sheet.

The stockbrokerage firms that sold DBSI to investors were obligated to conduct a *reasonable investigation* of DBSI before they sold it. The fact that any stockbrokerage firm sold DBSI securities is tantamount to proof that the brokerage firm never looked at DBSI's finances. No honest broker who looked at DBSI's finances would have sold DBSI securities.

This is also a theme that will repeat throughout this book. Stockbrokerage firms that sell private investments are required to conduct a reasonable investigation of the company whose securities they sell. Firms that sell investments in Ponzi schemes generally do not investigate at all.

There was one particular Ponzi scheme that was a little different and which I saw played out twice about ten years apart. In both cases, the high returns were supposedly generated by medical receivables that were purchased at a discount.

In the 1990s a company called **Towers Financial** raised hundreds of millions of dollars from investors. The funds were intended to purchase medical receivables from smaller, private hospitals. Investors were told that the medical insurance companies were paying slowly and that buying these receivables helped the cash flow of each small hospital.

Towers Financial allegedly bought the receivables at a discount of 8% and claimed to collect the bulk of them in ninety days as opposed to the thirty days that the hospitals needed. This supposedly allowed Towers to roll investors' money over four times per year generating more than a 30% return—more than enough to pay 18% to investors. The operators never actually bought any receivables and used money from newer investors to pay investors in its older funds.

What I especially remember about Towers is that they employed a group of actors who occupied desks in an office one floor below the corporate offices. When a brokerage firm showed up to investigate Towers, the executives would walk the party down one flight of stairs to the "bullpen."

Someone would call ahead and the actors would pretend to be hard at work on the telephones making *collections*. When the group left, everyone hung up their phone and laughed.

Beginning in 2003, a similar scam was repeated under the name of **Medical Capital Holdings**, which also claimed to be buying receivables from smaller hospitals and healthcare facilities. Once it allegedly bought the receivables of those companies, interests in the receivables were sold to investors in the form of private Medical Capital Notes.

Medical Capital Holdings issued more than **$2.2 billion** of Medical Capital Notes to some **20,000 investors** across the country. These notes were sold by stockbrokerage firms in almost every state.

By the time the SEC sued Medical Capital for fraud in July 2009, Medical Capital had almost $550 million in phony receivables on its books and had lost over $300 million on various loans that it did make. Meanwhile, the company had collected over $300 million in fees for managing the money-losing loans.

The bankruptcy receiver discovered that Medical Capital spent $4.5 million on a 118-foot yacht and another $18 million on an unreleased movie about a Mexican Little League team.

The stockbrokerage firms that sold Towers Financial securities or Medical Capital notes earned their commissions by finding people who were willing to write checks to become investors. None of these investors got a fair deal. Every one of them invested into a Ponzi scheme. Every one of them had their money stolen.

The individuals who organized and ran Medical Capital had previously had serious problems with insurance industry regulators. These problems were not disclosed to potential investors. That fact alone should have been a red flag to any stockbrokerage firm that had actually conducted a reasonable investigation of Medical Capital.

The firms that did not investigate Medical Capital sold $2 billion dollars worth of phony Medical Capital securities to about 20,000 people. Every investor suffered a substantial loss.

How could this have been avoided? Simply.

Ponzi schemes do not spend the money that they raise in the way they promise investors. Who keeps track of the money that a company raises and how it is spent? Auditors. Medical Capital and many of these other questionable investments had none.

Medical Capital refused to hire a reputable accounting firm to audit their books. That reason alone should have been enough for any reputable stockbrokerage to refuse to offer Medical Capital securities for sale to its customers.

Auditors play a crucial role in the public securities markets. They make certain that companies publicly report specific financial information about their business and their balance sheets. Auditors provide a transparency and a consistency in our evaluation of the firms who are seeking capital.

Audited financial statements are rare in the private securities market. That is partly because regulations governing the private sale of securities do not require audited statements for all private offerings. It is also because there is a presumption in the private markets that participants are more sophisticated and that they can fend for themselves.

A sophisticated investor, presumably, could determine whether or not a company was a Ponzi scheme by saying: *if you want my investment, open up your books so that I can verify that you will do what you say with my money*. No one would expect a company to comply with such a request from an individual investor, unless the investment was exceedingly large.

That is the role stockbrokerage firms are supposed to play. If these firms had done their job, those offerings would not have been made and those losses would not have occurred.

Hundreds of billions of dollars' worth of private placement investments are sold to non-institutional accredited investors every year. Only the stockbrokerage firms that sell these investments stand between these investors and fraud and unnecessary losses.

Many investors fail to realize that many private investments they are offered are similar to investments that they could make in the public securities market. Private investments will offer to pay you more and your broker will earn more for selling it to you.

Private investments are always considered to be speculative. If you are not willing to lose your money (and many people do) private investments are not for you.

CHAPTER VI
Private Placements

The US securities markets are among the best regulated and most transparent in the world. Businesses seeking investors can register their securities with the SEC and sell them to anyone they wish. At the same time, companies are allowed to raise funds in smaller, private offerings or private placements that are not required to be registered with the SEC.

These private offerings were historically sold to banks, insurance companies and large private investment funds. Because they are private transactions, these securities can be structured in a myriad of ways. Specific disclosures that would be made to investors in a public offering are not always present in a private offering.

The SEC staff reviews and comments upon the information and disclosures that are used in a public offering. No government agency reviews the offering materials used in a private placement.

Private placement offering materials frequently exaggerate the positives and discount the negatives about the investment. Too often, private placement offerings cross the line by making statements that are untrue or omitting important facts that investors would want to know. When they cross that line, they are committing fraud.

Hundreds of billions of dollars' worth of fraudulent private placements are sold every year.

Average mom and pop investors have generally been steered away from this market. Federal rules have historically provided limited access to high income or high net worth individuals, only.

The high income or high net worth individuals who are permitted to participate in these private offerings are called **accredited investors**. One principal purpose of the accredited investor concept is to identify people who can bear the economic risk of investing in these unregistered securities.

If you have a net worth of $1 million (exclusive of your home) or earn $200,000 per year ($300,000 with your spouse) you are automatically an ***accredited investor*** under the regulations that govern the issuance of these private securities.

As an accredited investor, you are deemed to be knowledgeable and sophisticated enough to consider an investment in a private placement. Make no mistake, you need to be a fairly sophisticated investor in order to understand many mainstream private placements.

Accredited investors are presumed to be sophisticated investors ***who can take care of themselves*** in the financial markets. The SEC rules classify *wealthy investors* as *sophisticated investors,* although in the real world one frequently has little to do with the other.

It is presumed that their wealth gives accredited investors access to information that would presumably allow them to make completely informed investment decisions. This presumption, that wealth equals investment sophistication, is the fallacy upon which many private placements are bought and sold.

It is also the reason why private placement offerings can be so problematic for investors. Sellers hide behind the fact that buyers are *deemed to be sophisticated* when many people clearly are not.

I taught freshman economics at a well-reputed business school. Very few of my clients who were accredited investors because of their financial position, and therefore deemed to be knowledgeable investors, could have passed my second mid-term examination.

I have represented more than one corporate executive, surgeon or software engineer and a few entertainers who frankly did not know the first thing about finance or investing. Each had lost more than $1 million by *trusting* some financial professional to steer them to the right investments.

If any of these people had understood what they were doing, not one of these supposedly sophisticated investors would have written a check for the investments that they actually made.

Each of these people met the income and net worth requirements to be *accredited investors.* In each case the broker recorded that they also met the standards to be considered to be *knowledgeable and sophisticated investors* as well, because those standards are the same.

Many retirees find themselves sitting across the desk from a financial professional who is recommending that they invest in a private placement. Hundreds of billions of dollars are raised every year to fund all kinds of real estate, oil and gas projects, new ventures, new technologies, films, franchises—businesses of every kind, here and abroad. Most of these securities will be sold to large banks, insurance companies and large funds. Some are expressly intended to be sold to smaller, individual accredited investors. All can be legitimate investments; some are not.

The private securities markets are subject to fewer regulations and fewer restrictions than are the public markets. This allows smaller companies to raise capital without too much cost. In practice, the lax regulations and the even more lax enforcement create an opportunity for scam artists and retirees to get together.

It should not surprise you that a great amount of fraud is targeted at people at the lower end of the scale that bottoms at a $1 million dollar net worth. People who retire with a $1 million net worth seem particularly susceptible to a sales pitch that includes: ***a bigger check every month.***

This is common, even though one would think that any retiree whose net worth was only one million dollars would not want to risk the loss of any significant portion of it.

Over the years, I became aware of unscrupulous financial professionals who helped customers cheat—i.e. falsify their income or net worth—so they could get in on one of these private placements. Qualifying investors as accredited when they are not is usually motivated by a big, fat commission that the financial professional will receive.

If a financial professional suggests that you over-estimate your income, net worth or any other important information on any form so that you will qualify to purchase any investment—*walk away.*

The ***sales pitch*** for a private placement will generally extol the benefits of pooling your funds with the funds of other investors so that you can invest in opportunities that would ***only be available to institutional investors***. People are told: ***The best deals are in the private securities market.***

The ***sale pitch*** will tell you how good the people behind this investment have been at making money for their investors. It is because they have such a ***fantastic track record*** of making money for people that you should ***hurry and get on board.***

Private placements often have a limited number of investors and can be structured to close quickly. That does not mean that you should not take the time to investigate before you invest. It means that the people who are asking for your money are making it difficult for you to appropriately evaluate the investment.

The sales pitch for private placements includes higher returns to investors generated by highly trained and successful business people. The sales pitch frequently notes that the investment was specifically structured or the business will be operated in such a way as to reduce normal investment or operational risks. Many private placements are presented as "reduced risk" investments or as "safe and suitable for retirees."

The sales pitch notwithstanding, a private placement is almost always a ***speculative*** investment. It may not perform as anticipated. It may be a total loss.

Private securities do not trade in an organized public securities market. Securities that you acquire in a private placement cannot be easily liquidated if you need the cash. Long-term illiquidity increases the risk of any investment because there is a greater opportunity for something adverse to occur, causing the investment to lose value.

If you are not prepared to lose the funds that you are investing in a private placement, you should not invest.

Speculative investments, like private placements, should only be offered to a limited number of investors—those who truly understand the investment that they are making and who are also ready, willing and able to lose their money should that come to pass.

No stockbroker or investment advisor should ever recommend a private placement investment to anyone who does not want to speculate with their funds and who is not prepared to lose their funds and in some cases, perhaps more. A great many financial professionals do just that.

Some financial firms and financial brokers specialize in selling *only* private placements because they pay significantly higher commissions than other financial products. Selling private placements, a stockbroker might earn a commission of 6%

or 8% or more all at once. Managing those same funds for you in a portfolio of stocks and bonds, the same broker or advisor might earn closer to 1% or 2% per year.

If a stockbrokerage firm could offer retirees an investment that paid a 6% or 7% or 8% annual return with little risk, people would seek them out. If these private placements could deliver that same return without risk, the stockbrokerage firms would not have to incentivize their salespeople with a 6% or 8% commission to sell them.

With every private placement offering, you should get a private placement memorandum **(PPM)**. A well-written PPM can be several hundred pages of legal documents and financial information, including charts, spreadsheets and graphs.

The PPM should contain all of the facts about the investment, the business behind it and the people who are asking for your money to fund and operate it, that any investor would want to know. The PPM is designed to protect those people and shield them from liability from you.

It is important for you to read and understand what you are being told. If you do not read the PPM or understand the transaction, the chances of you flushing your money away increase substantially.

Private placements are securities and can only be sold by firms and individuals who are registered with the SEC, specifically stockbrokers and Registered Investment Advisors.

One of the functions of stockbrokerage firms is to provide access to the capital markets for deserving businesses. It is up to the firms offering the investments to determine which companies are deserving of their customers' funds. The only way for a brokerage firm to determine which companies are deserving of funding is to investigate the company that will be receiving the money.

Stockbrokerage firms and Registered Investment Advisors that sell private placements are **required to conduct a reasona-**

ble, diligent investigation of the company before they offer it to investors. Specifically, they are required to ***verify the information*** in the PPMs that they are giving out.

In the industry, these are called due diligence investigations. As with any investigation, the devil is often in the details.

Inadequate investigations of private securities transactions were the source of a great many problems for investors in the last market cycle and crash. Some stockbrokerage firms simply refused to dedicate the time and money necessary to adequately investigate the companies and people to whom they were directing their customers' money.

I have seen a great many private placement investments implode. Some had the best pedigrees and were structured intelligently and with favorable costs and demographics. Many of these investments made at least some commercial sense at the time that they were offered, but not all.

In the early 1990s, many attorneys, myself included, brought claims on behalf of retirees who had been sold ***real estate limited partnerships*** by the largest and most reputable stockbrokerage firms in the industry at that time. Many of these partnerships were public with thousands of investors. Others were private placements.

Billions of dollars were lost when real estate markets pulled back and when many of the partnerships were exposed as being questionable from the outset.

There were so many claims involving ***real estate limited partnerships*** that had been sold by one firm that one federal court had to set up a special arbitration/mediation system to deal with the thousands of aggrieved investors. When it was all said and done, none of the investors got all of their money back and retirees, as a class, suffered a disproportionate amount of the losses.

What did we learn from all of those claims involving real estate limited partnerships from the early 1990s? What did we learn from the billions of dollars in losses suffered by retirees and other investors back then?

We certainly did not learn that real estate markets, like all markets, go up and down; or that markets that go up quickly, frequently come down—hard. If we had learned it then, we might have avoided the same problem and the much larger losses when the real estate market went up and came down again in the mid-2000s.

I have heard many financial professionals testify under oath that the losses that their customers sustained because of the real estate crash of 2008 were *unforeseeable.* When things go wrong, financial professionals frequently argue that they could not predict the future even though predicting the future is their stock in trade.

I have filed claims for people who had been sold *mainstream private placements* by *mainstream stockbrokerage firms* who specialized in these products. In many cases, the underlying investment was in real estate because a great many people think that 1) they really understand real estate investing and 2) real estate is a relatively safe investment and 3) real estate almost always goes up in value over time. If you believe that No. 2 and No.3 are true then No. 1 is necessarily false.

Many private placement investments, including those structured around real estate, are poorly structured and top-heavy with fees. The underlying property is often overvalued and sometimes properties are packaged for sale to groups of unsuspecting individual accredited investors because no one else would buy them.

Investors are entitled to the facts, good and bad, about the people who are managing the companies into which they are investing their money. Some people seem willing to embellish their resumes; more frequently, people leave out the bad things that they have done to prior investors.

I attended a presentation for an oil and gas investment back in the mid-1980s. The gentleman who made the presentation made a lot of promises that seemed questionable to me at the time and I did not invest. There were also a lot of senior citizens at the presentation and that concerned me as well.

Some years later, I learned that the investment had indeed failed and more than one of the investors had sued, claiming that they had been defrauded.

Fast-forward to 2008 and a client approached me to file a claim against a stockbroker who had sold him a private placement of interests in a self-storage facility in Alaska.

The same gentleman, who had held himself out as an experienced oil and gas producer, was now claiming to be an experienced real estate operator. There was no mention of the fact that investors in his previous venture thought that he had defrauded them when he took their money and had sued him.

His partner in this real estate venture had owned a financial firm in the 1990s that the SEC had alleged was actually owned by someone else. This partner had been sanctioned by the SEC for having an undisclosed principal at his firm. The sanction meant that he had not told the SEC the truth.

When I read through the PPM for the self-storage facility, I would have expected both the litigation alleging securities fraud and the SEC sanction would have been disclosed. Disclosure of these prior "bad acts" in the PPMs was clearly required. Neither of these specific bad acts was disclosed in this new PPM.

Between 2003 and 2006, these two individuals working together raised several hundred million dollars for about forty real estate projects, apartment buildings, office buildings and other commercial projects without ever telling their investors of their "checkered" pasts.

All of these sales were accomplished with the help of a number of stockbrokerage firms who clearly did not investigate the information in the PPMs that they were handing out.

I questioned the owner of one of these stockbrokerage firms at an arbitration hearing. His firm had sold over $1 billion worth of private placements in the 2005-2008 timeframe.

He testified that the firm employed one, part-time due diligence investigator who was expected to investigate as many as a dozen private placements per month. That does not seem to be an adequate allocation of resources with the intention to get the job done right.

At this firm and at many other stockbrokerage firms that specialized in private placements, *a reasonable investigation did not happen.* The due diligence officer just read the PPM and reviewed materials supplied by the company and signed off. The only real question asked was: *will this sell?*

The difference between these cursory reviews and a real investigation allowed a lot of fraudsters to scam thousands of retirees.

The type of due diligence investigation that is reasonable for a particular private placement will vary from one to the other, although there are some basic guidelines for an investigation of any security offering. Usually one person who knows what they are doing is managing a team of people with financial and accounting backgrounds and other special skills that may be necessary.

To bring this down to the simplest level, in one case a company failed to disclose that the roof of the building being syndicated to investors needed repair. No one had bothered to get the building inspected before they sold it to the investors or if they did, they made a decision not to tell the investors about the inspection before the closing. This led to expensive litigation and expensive repairs.

The investors borrowed the money to get the roof fixed and for the next few years the building will have a negative cash flow. Many of the investors in this building were expecting to receive checks every month from this investment. Instead they are making cash calls, sending money to the management company so that the building can cover its expenses until the new roof is paid off.

In my mind, no financial professional would ever sell a real estate investment that was essentially one office building to anyone without an independent physical inspection of the building. The stockbrokers' insurance company took the position that the sophisticated, accredited investors should have done more of an investigation of the property themselves and initially refused to settle.

Investors would not have been directed to this and many other fraudulent investments if the stockbrokerage firms had merely *verified* that the facts that they were telling their customers about these investments were true.

A reasonable investigation of a private placement is not necessarily complicated and the stockbrokerage firms are required to do it. Many do not even attempt to conduct an investigation or do it well.

After the 2008 crash once again exposed private placements as a source of significant investor losses and poor due diligence, the SEC passed rules to make it easier for firms to sell private placements by permitting companies that want to raise money to solicit potential investors directly.

If you take a step back and look at what happened, the financial services industry burned thousands of investors with private placements. The industry then helped the government change the rules to make it easier for the industry to find new customers.

The prior rule against the general solicitation of private placement investments prohibited sponsors from direct advertising for investors. With the new rules, expect to be inundated with ads for *great* real estate or energy investments that claim to pay 8% or 10% or more. Watch out for headlines that read: *Retirees, need steady income?*

Private placements and the private securities markets are an integral part of our capital formation system. But they are not for every investor and certainly not for most retirees who cannot afford to speculate with substantial sums.

Stockbrokerage firms that sell private placements would do well to consider an order from a retiree for an investment in a private placement to be an exception, not the rule.

Regulators should understand that they could save a lot of misery without damaging the capital formation system and still restrict sales of private placements to senior citizens.

I do not expect that this will happen.

I do expect that more and more companies will continue to seek capital in the private markets. Stockbrokers will continue to accept much higher than average commissions to raise that capital for them.

If every stockbrokerage firm actually conducted their business in accordance with the already existing industry rules that prohibits them from selling speculative securities to customers who do not want to speculate, this problem would substantially evaporate.

I do not expect that this will happen, either.

In the next few chapters I will look under the hood of several private placements that should never have been sold. A diligent investigation on the part of the stockbrokerage firms that sold these particular private placements would have saved a lot of people a lot of financial misery. Notwithstanding, thousands of customers lost billions of dollars in these and similar investments. These losses did not have to happen.

CHAPTER VII
The Pavilion

I wish to dissect two real estate private placement securities that were sold by a number of different stockbrokerage firms. They are excellent examples of very risky investments that were not marketed as very risky investments and which ensnared many retirees.

The purchase and operation of a substantial amount of commercial real estate, office and apartment buildings, strip malls, regional malls, industrial parks and agricultural property are often funded in the private securities markets.

Where the sale of a building to two or three investors might be nothing more than a run-of-the-mill real estate transaction, the sale of the same building to fifteen or twenty unrelated investors would likely be classified as a securities offering. The distinction is often determined by the way in which the transaction and legal documents are structured.

The **Pavilion** (not its real name) was a single, four-story office building located in a suburban neighborhood of a major Sunbelt city. The building itself was a Class A office building. It was in good repair and in a good neighborhood. It was located on a commercial boulevard near an upscale shopping mall with smaller retail clusters and other office buildings nearby.

Most of the tenants in the building were smaller local businesses and professional offices; small law, accounting and insurance firms; a dentist; a local charity and similar tenants. One tenant, which occupied a little more than 40% of the building, was the local sales office of a national company that had a triple-A credit rating. The Pavilion was almost fully occupied when it was offered to investors.

Interests in the company that owned the building were offered and sold to investors in the middle of 2005. The offering was made by an experienced real estate group **REG** (not its real name) whose business was to locate buildings like this one and essentially flip them to accredited investors through a stable of stockbrokerage firms with whom it had an interesting relationship.

Professional sponsors like REG create a pipeline of financial products for these firms to sell. That makes them as important to the firms as the firms are to them.

It is not unusual for a private placement sponsor to also sponsor events, conventions and golf tournaments for the firm's brokers or to provide other separate incentives that are never disclosed to the investors who pay for it all.

In one case, a broker blurted out: *"Of course I thought that he was a successful developer, I was at a party on his yacht."*

In this case, the Pavilion offering was sold to investors for $30 million. There was a $20 million mortgage and about forty investors put up various shares of $10 million in cash.

Each of the investors in this project had previous experience as a real estate investor. The investment was specifically structured to accommodate investors who were selling other properties so that they might take advantage of a section of the Internal Revenue Code (IRC) that would allow them to defer capital gains taxes that they might otherwise have had to pay.

As with all sections of the IRC, in order to obtain the tax deferral the taxpayer had to comply with the regulations. One of those regulations required taxpayers who sold appreciated real estate to swap into another real estate investment very quickly.

To comply with the regulations, these investors needed to locate and identify a new real estate investment within six weeks of the time that they sold their prior property. With a large, complex real estate transaction, this is often hard to do.

As importantly, the investors are limited to properties that happen to be on the market during the short window when they need to find a "replacement" property. This can also be problematic.

The SEC is always telling investors to take the time to *investigate before you invest*. This is always sound advice. The IRS's regulation that required *quick action* on the part of the investors in order to obtain tax deferrals was part of a recipe for disaster.

Tens of thousands of investors were sold similar tax-deferred investments without really investigating the investments themselves because the regulations did not give them adequate time to do so, assuming that they had known what to do. Just like the boiler-room operators, the IRS regulations created a sense of urgency so that investors were asked to act without adequate thought or review.

REG was owned by two partners: one had been involved in various real estate ventures over a period of 25 years; the other had been a real estate attorney who had originally been a partner at a regional law firm.

By 2005, REG presented itself as an established, professional organization. It offered several professionally produced glossy brochures and slide shows. REG touted its track record with a chart showing how well each of their prior real estate offerings had paid investors.

In addition to the glossy brochures, the offering package for this investment contained a thick **PPM**. The PPM was hundreds of pages long, full of legal documents, charts and graphs. There was also a sheaf of contracts and legal documents that each investor had to sign in order to purchase these securities.

I have personally helped prepare more than 100 PPMs. Very few of the investors who purchased interests in the Pavilion and the thousands of private placements like it actually understand the nuances of the legal documents that the PPMs contain or summarize. Most investors never get past the glossy brochures.

The PPM for the Pavilion contained a chart showing that the 40 prior projects that REG had sold to investors had all made those investors money. The average investor in this particular private placement (I have personally spoken with about half of them) would not know where to begin to ***verify*** the information contained on the prior performance chart. Only the firm's auditors could actually have enough information to do so.

REG, like many other similar real estate sponsors, touted its prior successes. People want to invest with people who have a proven record of success. A simple, direct question: was the chart of REG's prior performance that was given to prospective investors in the Pavilion accurate?

In the case of REG the prior performance table was not audited nor was it accurate. No stockbrokerage firm that sold interests in the Pavilion to investors apparently questioned the information that the chart contained. When I conducted my own research before I filed our first claims on behalf of investors, it became apparent that REG had at least one large failure during the prior real estate cycle that had simply been left off the prior performance chart given to these investors.

When the sponsor of a private placement investment intentionally leaves out important facts that make the information that you are given misleading, you should invest your money elsewhere.

If you become aware that people with whom you are dealing are willing to mislead you in order to take your money, do not accept any excuses—***move on.***

The Pavilion was a speculative investment. The ownership of the building could have been structured in such a way as to provide less risk and more protection for the investors' equity. This particular investment was structured in such a way as to exacerbate and shift many of those risks to investors, largely to increase the profit for REG.

The tenant with the triple-A credit rating which had been occupying 40% of the building vacated in 2009 after paying a $1 million lease termination penalty. Rather than use those funds to build out the space for a new tenant, REG distributed the million dollars to the investors as if the tenant were still there. That, of course, left the building with no funds to remodel the 40% of the building that was now empty should they locate another tenant.

It did allow the real estate group to maintain the façade that all was still well into 2010. As long as the investors were still getting checks, they were not suspicious of any problems. Getting a check every month just like always, has the effect of lulling investors to sleep. As long as they were getting checks, there was no reason for investors to think that they had been defrauded in the first place.

In 2010 the statutes of limitations for the fraud that the real estate group had committed when they offered these securities in mid-2005 began to run out.

A new tenant was not located and the mortgage could not be paid. The building was worth less than the $20 million dollar mortgage, making refinancing impossible. The mortgage holder foreclosed on the building, wiping out the investors equity—a total loss of the $10 million that the investors had put up less than five years earlier.

REG will tell you, correctly, that the risk that this might happen is clearly set forth in the PPM under the heading "Risk Factors." A well-written PPM generally covers these contingencies.

At the same time REG, and just about every other real estate group that packaged and sold these investments, will tell you that the drop in the real estate market that began in 2007 and continued into 2009 was **unprecedented.** They believe that investors' losses were the result of market action that no one could have anticipated nor guarded against. Nothing could be further from the truth.

The drop in real estate prices during this period was extensive and was felt across many markets. Overall, the foreclosure rate for similar office buildings increased from previous years but was never higher than 8% nationally, meaning that the real estate crisis did not force 92% of similar buildings into foreclosure.

Some markets were affected more than others, especially those where there had been a sharp run-up in real estate prices during the preceding boom years. Sunbelt cities such as the one in which the Pavilion was located had seen a boom in real estate prices in the years prior to 2005.

That real estate prices in the city where the Pavilion was located came down sharply should have surprised no one. It is was exactly what had occurred in the prior real estate cycle, causing the project that REG left off their prior performance chart to go into foreclosure.

The offering package for this investment also included a spreadsheet showing ***projected revenues*** based upon existing leases and anticipated expenses for the building. The spreadsheet showed that both income and expenses were likely to rise over time with inflation. After seven to ten years, the building was projected to be sold at a profit.

Stockbrokerage firms that sell these investments are required to have a reasonable basis for the projections that they give to their customers. Statistics was not my favorite subject in college but I do know that the projections that accompanied the Pavilion offering were based upon fallacious assumptions and lacked any statistical validity. These particular projections assumed continued growth in the Sunbelt city's real estate market without any correction or abatement for the ten years after 2005.

By 2005 the real estate market in and around that particular Sunbelt city had been very hot for almost a decade. It was that fact that was used to project increasing rents and increasing values for another ten years.

There was no fundamental reason that this market, which had been that hot for that long, should expect real estate values to continue to only go up. Whoever made this projection did so because they wanted it to be true, not because they had any real facts to support it.

Instead of cashing out in ten years, the forty investors in this investment each lost 100% of their investment in less than six years—in part because the real estate market did what real estate markets do—it pulled back. This result was duplicated by similar private placement investments that had also projected a very rosy future in markets that no one should have predicted would be rosy.

Let me offer the obvious: **projections that accompany any investment will always show that investors can expect a reasonable or substantial profit.** The spreadsheet for the Pavilion showed the building would be sold at a profit in seven to ten years in a real estate market that had gone up every year in between.

Every investor in the Pavilion with whom I spoke had gone over the projections with their financial professional. More than one was told: ***worst case, you will earn half as much.*** None were asked to consider that they might experience a total loss in six years.

The most important part of the ***spreadsheet projection*** was that it showed how the building could be operated so profitably that it could also pay the investors ***a return on their investment*** every year, starting immediately. In the case of the Pavilion, the investment was projected to payout an 8% return to investors in the early years, which would increase to over 11% as time went on. The increase was based upon the idea that rents would steadily increase, year after year.

You can see why retirees were drawn to an investment that promised an 8% return in early years, an 11% return later on and a substantial profit on their money when the property was ultimately sold.

The 8% and 11% projections were on the cover of the glossy brochure for the Pavilion that was handed to prospective investors, in **very big, bold type.** These retired investors were concerned first and foremost about the size of their monthly checks.

REG chose to present projections as part of its sales presentation. The projections should have accurately reflected what would happen if things do not go according to the best-case scenario.

Many projections for office building investments like the Pavilion fail to account for deferred maintenance. Few test for the adequacy of reserves or take into account the effects of extended vacancies on profitability and returns. Even fewer consider whether or not new, competing buildings are being built in the same area that will compete for tenants and which may lower rents.

All too often, projections that accompany private placements are part of the sales pitch and not part of any legitimate analysis of the investment. Questionable spreadsheets are commonplace in some segments of the private placement market. **Beware of projections that look too good; they frequently disappoint.**

In the late 1980s one of the largest national stockbrokerage firms offered an investment in a residential community development in Orange County, California. The investment bankers who had put the investment package together projected that the houses would be built and sold according to a schedule that called for about 300 units to be built and sold every year. There was little doubt that if built, there was a healthy market of prospective buyers and those 300 sales per year could have been achieved.

The investment bankers in New York who packaged this investment and who produced those projections did not account for the fact that Orange County had placed a restriction on new residential water hookups because there had been several years of drought. Other developers were clamoring for those same hookups and 30-50 houses per year for this development would have been much more realistic if they wanted the houses to have water and occupancy permits.

The water hookup limit was only discovered after the firm had raised enough money to build the first 300 houses. The stockbrokerage firm settled with investors who had been misled. I always thought that this was more of an honest mistake than a premeditated fraud. In every case, however, **projections need to be based in reality**.

In the case of the Pavilion the people behind the real estate group that offered the investment misled investors because they put out a prior performance table that failed to show their prior failures. They also put out projections that had no basis in fact. They did not do so by accident. REG took in more than $1.5 million in profits and fees on the day that this offering closed.

If a stockbrokerage firm had caught REG fudging the numbers on its own past performance table, the obvious question should be: ***what else did they fudge?*** Firms that sold interests in the Pavilion just looked at the prior performance table and the projections, assumed they were accurate, and never really checked.

Legitimate stockbrokerage firms that actually investigate the private placements that they sell would have caught the fact that there were transactions in this sponsor's past that they did not want to disclose. In many cases, the lack of disclosure alone would have been enough for a legitimate stockbrokerage firm to refuse to sell offerings sponsored by REG.

But that is not why these investors lost money.

The Pavilion failed primarily because the investors paid too much for the investment in the first place. These investors paid a total of $30 million. They would have needed to sell the building for at least $30 million (plus exit fees and commissions) to break even.

At the time that the investors made their purchase, in mid-2005, the building had an appraised value of just a little over $25 million. REG had recently purchased the property for close to that price, added $1.5 million to the purchase price as their profit, repackaged the property as a security with costs and commissions and flipped it to the investors for $30 million.

REG had never operated the building before it sold it to investors. Everything that REG knew about the Pavilion came from information supplied to them by the prior owners. They passed that information onto the prospective investors without verifying whether the prior owner was telling the whole truth about anything.

The appraised value of $25 million in 2005 was significantly higher than the construction cost of the building, which was about $14 million when it was completed in 2002. The $30 million cost to investors in 2005 was probably twice the replacement cost of the building at the time. Other office buildings were being planned and built in the same general area, which would increase the competition for tenants.

Obviously these investors would have been better served if they had bought the building for the $25 million appraised value, which was the price that REG paid. The additional $5 million included REG's profit of $1.5 million, $500,000 to the lawyers and accountants who put the offering documents together and $3 million in brokerage commissions to the brokers who sold this $25 million building to the investors for $30 million.

Neither REG nor the stockbrokerage firms that raised the money took any risk nor brought any real value to this transaction. They added $5 million to the total cost of the investment just because they restructured this investment from a real estate transaction into a securities transaction. They put that $5 million of the investors' funds—about one half of the total amount that they raised from investors—into their own pockets.

REG also built in several layers of fees for management services that the investors did not need. This provided REG with a continuing income stream from each property that it packaged and sold. It also maintained its position as the operator of each building so that anything that was wrong, which should have been disclosed, could remain hidden.

That is the point with many private placements—a lot of commissions and fees with very little additional value. The resulting investment cost investors significantly more than the intrinsic or market value of the property. When you pay too much for a property in an up market, and that market turns down, it is easy to get underwater, especially when you need high rents to justify the higher price.

In this case, about forty investors lost $10 million. $5 million of that $10 million was booked as profit by REG and the brokers who had originally told investors how lucky the investors were to be able to invest in a project sponsored by REG.

In theory, these forty investors are supposed to be sophisticated enough to have spotted problems with this private placement before they invested. In reality, they paid $30 million for a building that was worth $25 million. How sophisticated could they actually have been? At least the investors were told that this was speculative investment.

It could have been much worse. The next private placement was not labeled as a speculative investment, was far more complex and difficult to analyze and was sold to a lot more people.

CHAPTER VIII

The Construction Investment Fund

There are many real estate companies and real estate funds and trusts that trade on the stock exchanges and in the public securities markets. You can find investments in apartment buildings, office buildings, medical offices and much more. Some are structured to pass through their income to investors. Some only pay investors when the property is sold.

The finances and management of these companies and funds are transparent because they are public. Any financial information that any investor would need to decide whether or not to invest is readily available because the information is on file with the SEC.

This is not true of securities issued in the private securities market. In the public markets, investors can limit their losses if things go bad with an immediate sale. This is not true of private securities either. So, why would you want to put your money into a private fund?

I call the second real estate private placement investment that I want to dissect the **Construction Investment Fund or CIF** (not its real name). **CIF** answered that question by offering 10% returns while claiming to be a lower risk fund.

About 4000 people followed their stockbroker's recommendation and pumped about $500 million into this fund. **Low risk? 10% return? Why not?**

CIF was not like other private real estate funds and trusts that are sold to retirees, which provide regular income. In other funds, the tenants in the properties pay rent every month. If the operation of the properties is profitable, then the excess of the rents over the expenses can be distributed to investors.

CIF's business plan was to make short-term construction loans. It was operated by a small mortgage brokerage company, also in a Sunbelt city. CIF provided capital for loans that the mortgage broker originated, primarily to fund the construction of new homes in the Southwest. These loans were supposed to be made to larger, more established developers who were building out upscale residential communities.

Construction loans are at the riskier end of real estate lending. Lenders who specialize in construction loans generally take care to manage and minimize their risks. CIF bragged about how many different steps it had taken to limit and mitigate the risks of its business.

CIF told investors that they had a number of safeguards in place to make certain that the loans it was making with the investors' money would be paid back. They continually claimed that every developer that had ever borrowed from CIF had paid off their loan when due. That *fact,* like many others, was simply not true.

The sales materials for CIF told potential investors that the developers who borrowed from the fund could have gone to traditional lenders for construction financing but that traditional lenders were too slow. The mortgage brokers behind CIF and their clients did not want to wait for traditional lenders so they underwrote the loans themselves and offered the loans to the investors' through the CIF fund.

CIF claimed to be ***over-collateralized*** on every loan that it made. CIF claimed to have ***independent appraisals*** to back up the values they were assigning to the collateral. Because it was a private lender, CIF could ask developers to add additional parcels and their own homes to the collateral and stated that it did so, on every loan.

CIF claimed that these loans were made for a ***very short term*** usually only twelve to eighteen months. The business plan for the developers was to borrow the money, build the homes, sell the homes and repay the loan. That was another reason that developers purportedly did not mind adding additional collateral because they were only tying up that collateral for a short time.

Finally, CIF claimed to have a ***personal guarantee*** from the developer who was behind every project that was being financed. The guarantee was supposed to be for the entire amount of the loan, not just potential deficiencies.

The sales brochures said that CIF only dealt with wealthy, successful builders who were experienced and who had made personal fortunes developing just these types of upscale residential communities. CIF allegedly got credit reports on each of the borrowers and copies of their personal tax returns and bank statements before they made the loans.

Unlike many other private funds, CIF also offered a limited redemption feature. CIF would accept redemption requests up until a certain date each quarter. The fund would set aside a certain amount for redemptions, and depending on how many other people wanted to liquidate their shares, it could take between one and six months to get your money.

Nothing about CIF suggested anything other than the fund operators had done quite a lot to secure the loans that the fund was making. Nothing in the sales literature or in the PPM suggested that this was a speculative investment or that investors might lose all or most of their money. Stockbrokers who sold the fund were paid a 2% commission, not the 8% or more they would expect with a more speculative real estate security.

The only outward sign that the investment was speculative was the fact that it paid investors 10% per year. With the 2% commission and the loan origination fees that the developers were paying, the actual loans cost the developers 14%-16%.

This was certainly not the rate that wealthy individuals making personal guarantees would be likely to pay in order to borrow money at a bank. This was explained away as being the price of speed and flexibility of dealing with a private lender. The developers could break ground sooner if they did not have to wait for the bank and its overworked lending staff and loan committees.

The fund told this story until it closed in the fall of 2008. By then CIF had grown to more than $500 million dollars and had thousands of investors. CIF was, after all, paying a 10% annual dividend. Many investors were retirees who were depending upon those monthly checks.

In October 2008, CIF abruptly stopped taking in new investors, stopped making loans, stopped all distributions and ceased to offer or fund redemptions. The fund continued to remind investors that its goal all along had been to never lose investors' money. These losses, they claimed, were caused by unprecedented events in the financial markets.

These unprecedented events in the financial markets apparently caused each and every one of the construction loans that CIF had made to default. Within several months of closing, CIF reported that 97% of its loans had defaulted. Roughly $400 million or 80% of those investors' funds in CIF were lost.

It now appears that CIF told lie after lie about how the fund was operating. If any of the stockbrokerage firms that had sold

CIF had investigated it first, they probably would have sold something else. CIF should not have passed muster.

What about the fact that these were short-term loans? If the average term of the loans CIF was making was 18 months or less, then it is reasonable to expect that some of the loans were more than half paid off when the fund closed. CIF would have had to have been making new loans until well into 2008 for the fund to lose this much in value. It was.

By the time the fund stopped lending, many of its outstanding loans were already in trouble. Because it continued to make monthly distributions for most of 2008, CIF had very little cash left. CIF needed every dollar that did come in to continue paying the executives who had caused all of the problems in the first place.

What about the fact that these loans were over-collateralized with independent appraisals? When the dust settled it became apparent that the fund was left with vacant land surrounded by more vacant land, all in subdivisions that had lots and lots of empty lots.

The appraisals that were done at the time the loans were made were based upon what the property would be worth *after* the homes were built. These *as-built* appraisals are not uncommon in construction lending, but that does not mean that traditional lenders will make a construction loan based upon the as-built value.

It also became apparent that the market for homes in upscale subdivisions in this portion of the Southwest had long peaked. CIF was already restructuring loans in 2006 and 2007 *because the developers who had borrowed the money could not sell the homes that they were building.*

By restructuring the loans the fund was also able to brag that it had never had a default. These prior problems came as a surprise to people who put in their money after 2006 and 2007 and who were led to believe that every borrower had paid back their loan to CIF without any problem.

What about the personal guarantees? We prosecuted claims for customers against about a dozen stockbrokerage firms that raised the bulk of the $500 million dollars for CIF. In due course, we asked each of the firms about the personal guarantees.

Each of these firms had passed along the sales literature that CIF had produced, extolling the safety of the fund because its loans were secured with personal guarantees from the wealthy, successful developers themselves. Not one of the stockbrokerage firms had actually seen a guarantee signed by a single one of the borrowers, nor could they produce one.

Five years later, the fund has never reported that a single loan had been paid off because a single developer had made good on their personal guarantee.

There are all types of personal guarantees. Some do not require payment until the underlying collateral is sold. Some do not apply if the company files for bankruptcy protection. Others *only* apply if the company files for bankruptcy protection.

Exactly what personal guarantees did CIF have in place to protect investors? It is clear that they did not provide the kind of security for the loans that the sales literature implied. None of the stockbrokerage firms I questioned actually knew what the guarantees looked like or if they actually existed.

Universally, the brokers that sold CIF believed the sales pitch that they had been given without asking any questions. It was the same sales pitch that they passed along to the unsuspecting customers. It was the same sales pitch that promised personal guarantees from wealthy developers that did not exist, as well as a lot of collateral that had limited market value.

It would have been reasonable for any stockbrokerage firm to look at the personal guarantees and the appraisals just to verify what the sales materials were saying. Every one of the stockbrokerage firms that helped to raise the $500 million should have been able to testify: *Here, we looked at half a dozen guarantees and they all looked solid to us.*

Not one firm could make that statement because not one of these firms had actually asked to see any of the personal guarantees. To this day, no brokerage firm can offer proof that the guarantees existed or offer any explanation why the guarantors did not make good.

A good independent appraisal is essential in any real estate financing. A bank lending money on commercial real estate will typically use its own appraiser for every transaction. Stockbrokerage firms frequently accept an appraisal provided by the company seeking funds. Appraisals can always be a problem because they are somewhat subjective.

In one recent case, involving a property in Texas, we discovered two appraisals for the exact same property that were identical from page two through the end. One appraised value (the appraisal that went to the bank) was $1.5 million less than the appraisal that was given to the investors. The appraisals were the same document: same appraiser, same signature and the same date. The only difference was the two first pages with two different appraised values.

The appraisal that valued the property for less was addressed to the loan committee at a bank that was considering the mortgage. The one with the higher appraised value was addressed to the stockbrokerage firms selling to retail accredited investors.

It is a felony to make a false or fraudulent appraisal to a bank to induce them to make a loan—a felony that does get prosecuted. As a practical matter, the penalty for an appraiser adding $1.5 million to the value of this building, even with the intent to defraud the investors in this offering, is virtually nil.

In the case of CIF, the appraisals used were based upon the anticipated sales price of the houses. It is not that the appraisals for CIF should not have included *as-built* valuations. A lender wants to know that the homes being built can be sold at a price to cover the loan.

Lending against collateral that has not been built can be very risky and can lead to loans backed by nothing more than raw land which was the case with CIF. Traditional lenders cover that risk with insurance—what is known as a completion bond. If the developer cannot finish the project, the bonding company comes in and pays for the uncompleted construction so that the homes can be liquidated as finished products.

In the case of CIF the absence of a completion bond for each loan left the risk of the uncompleted homes with the investors. Anyone who was familiar with construction lending would have asked about the non-completion risk and how it was covered before they agreed to sell this product to investors.

That, in a nutshell, is the problem. Many of these stockbrokerage firms that sold CIF and which sell other private placements today do not have the personnel or staff capable of conducting a reasonable investigation of a sophisticated real estate transaction.

At many firms these same investigators look into many types of real estate programs as well as oil and gas and other private financing programs that the firm offers. It is easy to see why the firms get into trouble. The firms lack the expertise to investigate the investments that they are selling and decline to spend what it takes to acquire that expertise. The losses that the customers of these firms suffered can be traced to that fact.

Many of the firms that sold CIF did no investigation at all. CIF actual sent out a due diligence kit which purported to include key documents that the stockbrokerage firms should have reviewed—if they had bothered. The firms put the documents in their files so that they could convince a regulator that they actually did something. The something that they did was put paper in their files.

That kit told the firms what CIF wanted the firms to know. If the firms had looked under the hood themselves, they might have gotten the whole story.

CIF was never a low risk investment. Even though the PPM did not contain the disclosure that the investment was speculative, investors lost 80% of their money. A careful review of the CIF fund's operations and the loans that it actually made would have confirmed this fact for all concerned.

No ethical and compliant stockbrokerage firm should have handed an investor a brochure that said CIF was a low risk investment. That pretty much tells you how I feel about the firms that did.

CHAPTER IX
Oil and Gas and Other Energy-Related Scams

Just as there are a variety of real estate investments, so too there are a myriad of ways that you can invest in the oil and gas industry in the public securities markets.

Anyone can invest in companies that not only drill for oil or gas, but also companies that own pipelines and transporters, refineries and traders. These securities are liquid because they trade on the exchanges or NASDAQ. The financial information for these investments is public and always audited.

Oil and gas investments in the private securities markets frequently have none of these attributes. They are always speculative and often fraudulent.

Oil and gas investments differ significantly from real estate investments. With real estate investments you can usually visit the site or building, speak with the current tenants and investigate the local market before you invest. You can see what you are buying.

With oil and gas, how much is underground is often based upon the opinion of a petroleum engineer, never on a visual assessment. This is not an exact science.

Even investments in producing oil wells can be considered to be speculative because the one certainty about oil wells is that at some point they stop producing.

There have always been hucksters involved in oil and gas finance. There have been bad deals and dishonest operators involved since commercial production began after the Civil War.

Court cases involving phony oil investments appeared in increasing numbers in the 1870s and continue to this day. It seems that investors can always be seduced into parting with their money if they can be persuaded that they are investing in the next gusher.

If you invest in the exploration of new fields and new wells, they can always come up dry. Exploratory drilling is at the riskiest end of the spectrum of oil and gas investments. Even when investors know that they are taking a substantial risk that they will lose their money, promoters can still find other ways to cheat them.

I am aware of one group of promoters who raised enough money to drill ten new oil wells, all of which they reported to be dry holes. Their investors were not surprised because these were brand new wells in a brand new field and everyone understands that people can typically drill a lot of oil wells before they find any oil.

Five years later this group was forced into bankruptcy court over another bad oil deal and it was disclosed that four of the original ten wells had been pumping oil all along. The promoters just never paid the proceeds to the original investors.

Retirees are more frequently solicited to invest in companies that develop existing fields. They are told that they have a better chance of striking oil in a field that is already producing. They are told that there is less risk because they will be attempting to tap into an existing pool of oil that has already been identified.

Oil and gas offerings often claim that they are about to strike oil or gas and they just need some investment to pay for *final drilling and well completion.* Please stop and ask yourself: Why would a company that is already in the oil business and about to strike oil, need to come to you for financing?

Drilling is often done on what is called a turnkey basis, meaning that the driller gets a fixed price for drilling the well or wells. A promoter may own the drilling company or hire a driller at far less than the cost that is represented to investors, while pocketing the difference. The promoter makes money from your investment even if the well comes up dry.

Where the money goes once it is turned over to the promoters is always a concern. Unlike construction financing, which is parceled out in stages as construction is completed, promoters of oil and gas investments often get all of the proceeds of the offering up front with little oversight or controls.

Generally, an experienced petroleum engineer or geologist will have made a determination that this company is drilling for oil in the right place. You should expect to get a copy of their report as part of any private placement offering. It is always preferable if the report is from a reputable independent third-party engineer or geologist. Understand that no company seeking your investment will ever hand you a report that does not suggest the potential for success.

You should also expect to see an audit of reserves or an independent reserve report. The use of terms such as "reserves" makes it sound like a sure thing. Reserves in the oil and gas industry are not so certain and can vary quite a lot.

Reserves can be "proved," "probable" or "possible." Proved reserves are relatively certain. Probable and possible reserves can mean a 50% to 10% chance of extracting the estimated amount. You can see why you would want to have the reserve amounts reviewed by a competent professional or audited by the firms' accountants.

Oil and gas investments are frequently sold based upon news or trends. A cold winter, for example, may lead people to believe that increased demand will increase heating oil prices. Energy prices are especially vulnerable to political events that may come on suddenly.

Crude oil, heating oil, gasoline and other refined petroleum products trade on the commodities exchanges where people spend a significant amount of effort attempting to identify price trends. I have heard more than one stockbroker testify that he sold an oil or gas investment to a retired couple because *the time was right*. For many retirees, it almost never is.

Assume for a moment that the broker actually understood the intricacies of the international energy markets. Even if his assertion had some foundation, I would always ask: *if you thought the price of oil or gas was going up in the medium or long-term, why not just buy shares in Conoco or Chevron?*

The oil and gas industry has also developed a unique way of carving up the risks and rewards of drilling and development and those of the landowners and leaseholders into *rights* and *interests*. Some people may own the land, others may own the mineral rights, others the drilling or development rights, and there can be royalties and other interests in the actual production—if there is any.

In Texas, the Railroad Commission keeps track of all of these interests for every property in the state. In other jurisdictions, the system can be far less organized. It can take an experienced oil and gas attorney to sort out all of these rights and interests. A full report of all interest holders is essential to determine who else will get paid if the well is successful. It should help an investor understand exactly what they are buying and how and when they get paid.

Is there a prior history of drilling where you are drilling? If someone previously drilled in the same spot or near it, how much did they get out and what makes you think you can get any more out? If the area proved dry before or has not been drilled, why do you think that there is something there?

A lot of new oil and gas is found in the United States today because of improved ways of drilling, such as hydraulic fracturing (i.e., fracking) and horizontal drilling. These improvements often require specialized expertise and may have a significant cost.

One repeated scam is a sales pitch that suggests that a large company had drilled in a particular field in the past but had abandoned it. You are asked to fund more drilling in the same field *with a newer technology* that will allow you to extract oil that Exxon or Conoco could not. Be very careful. If the new technology were so good, assume that Exxon would be there.

With oil and gas investments there is much that you cannot see and much that you do not know. It is often absolutely necessary to hire a qualified expert to help you evaluate a private oil or gas investment. You should expect that any stockbroker selling private oil and gas investments will have access to that expertise and will have experts evaluate any oil and gas investment before it is offered to you.

In one recent case, a Texas company called **Striker Petroleum** raised about $60 million to *rework* some older wells. After a while, the company that they had hired to do the drilling went bankrupt and it took a while to unravel the mess. In the meantime, the investors got no payments because the funds flowed through the Bankruptcy court.

Striker made a deal with the investors to pay them a fixed 12% per year instead of a variable amount based upon the flow and sale of oil. But Striker still did not have the income to make the payments; so Striker borrowed the money.

After it knew about the cash flow problems, Striker raised another $60 million by issuing a series of debentures. These debentures were supposed to be collateralized by specific assets, which were supposed to be entrusted to an independent

Trustee. In early 2009, the SEC froze all of Striker's assets when it became apparent that the Trustee had never been truly independent and the assets collateralizing these debentures may have been owned by someone else.

In the early 1990s a firm called **Kinlaw Securities** operated as a boiler room. Salesmen told scripted lies to random calling lists of wealthy potential investors. Where Stratton Oakmont and other boiler rooms sold shares in new companies and new technologies, Kinlaw Securities only sold stakes in the oil drilling projects of its sister company, Kinlaw Oil Corp. The company operated out of Dallas, Texas.

The fraud was easy to prove. Boiler room salesmen promised investors the potential of a 500% return. They told investors that Kinlaw almost never came up with a dry hole. Right there any investor should have been very suspicious. Some were not.

The SEC tried to shut them down, alleging that Kinlaw's sales pitch had defrauded investors out of about $125 million.

As I mentioned with Stratton Oakmont, I try to take notice when other lawyers handle a difficult legal problem well. Part of Kinlaw's defense was that it had not sold securities but partnership interests in various business ventures.

After several years of legal battles, the courts sided with Kinlaw and threw out the SEC complaint. The court held that the *interests* that Kinlaw sold in each of its drilling programs amounted to partnerships because the investors had some input into how the business was run.

If you buy a security, like shares of AAPL, you do not get to tell AAPL how to do anything that might affect the running of its business or its balance sheet. Investors in Kinlaw programs could exercise some amount of control—enough so that the court deemed them to be partners, not shareholders.

The investors had all been defrauded. They had all been promised ridiculous returns and each had heard false statements about Kinlaw's spotless track record. But because of the way in which the investments were structured, the anti-fraud provisions and remedies that the securities laws provide were not available. Investors could not recoup their money. Kinlaw essentially got away with its theft.

The original SEC complaint against Mr. Kinlaw and his companies was filed in 1993 and the Court's opinion denying the SEC jurisdiction over the investments came down in 1999.

In the interim, Mr. Kinlaw moved from Texas to Colorado. According to the Colorado Securities Commission, he sold another $300 million in partnership interests in various drilling programs, making similar exaggerated claims. A court subsequently told the Colorado Securities Commission that it did not have jurisdiction over these sales, either.

More recently, a phony oil investment that was sold to many retirees who were hoping for higher income was packaged and presented by **Provident Asset Management.** Between 2006 and 2009, Provident sold preferred stock and limited partnership interests (which were clearly securities) in a series of 23 private placements offered by its sister company, Provident Royalties, LLC.

Instead of a boiler room full of salespeople on telephones, Provident enlisted about fifty stockbrokerage firms nationwide who raised just under $500 million from thousands of individual accredited investors. Many of these investors were retirees as well.

The sales materials for the Provident Royalties' programs promised investors returns of up to 18% per year. The PPM promised that the funds raised through each offering would be used to purchase various interests in all aspects of the oil and gas business.

Provident Royalties promised to segregate the funds from each of their programs, one from the other. They promised to limit the offering and administrative costs of each program to no more than 14% of the amount that they raised. This included almost 10% in commissions and fees to the retail brokers and stockbrokerage firms that sold it. They promised to pay investors 1½ % per month from revenues derived from the royalties on the interests that they said that they would purchase.

None of these promises were true. Provident operated as a Ponzi scheme. Investor funds that had been segregated were freely moved from one account to another. They were used to pay dividends and to return funds to earlier investors so Provident looked successful.

Provident handled more than one-half billion dollars of investors' money. None of the stockbrokerage firms that sold it thought that auditors should be hired just to keep the company on the up and up.

I do not want you to think that oil or gas exploration or production are the only type of energy-related investments that are being sold or that they are the only place that you will find scams and scam artists. I also want to note the fact that retirees are not the only people who get burned in the private securities markets.

Everyone knows that there is an ongoing revolution in the energy business involving everything from windmills to ethanol to fusion reactors. Investment "opportunities" in alternative energy industries abound. Scam artists are taking full advantage.

In 2012, the SEC brought an action against a stockbrokerage firm based in Chicago called **Advanced Equities**. The firm specialized in raising funds for companies that had been funded and nurtured by professional venture capitalists. Advanced Equities provided the later stage financing to get these companies ready to go public. It dealt with some of the premier venture capital firms in Silicon Valley and elsewhere.

At one point Advanced Equities was having difficulty raising funds for a company in an alternative energy business. An

Advanced Equities executive apparently walked into a conference room full of salespeople and told everyone who would listen that the company had just signed an order from a government agency that would be worth $1 billion.

Was it true? No. But the salespeople apparently believed him and told potential investors about the big new order. The offering sold out. It is that easy to commit securities fraud.

There is always a proliferation of investments available with alternative energy producers or alternative energy companies. If you were to put the offering materials for two dozen of these investments side by side, you would begin to get a sense of the competing claims and the divergent facts that support those claims.

Discerning which companies are likely to succeed and which are not is what stockbrokerage firms are supposed to do for you. Remarkably, some firms will make that determination without having a qualified engineer express an opinion on the technology that will be used.

Many people actually believe that they are sophisticated enough that they can effectively evaluate a private placement offering after only reading the sales materials and listening to the sales presentation. Most individual investors (and many professional investors) do not know what questions to ask or even where to begin to detect fraud in a private placement offering.

Let me offer you my thoughts.

CHAPTER X

So You Still Want to Buy a Private Placement?

Historically, SEC rules prohibited advertising or general solicitation of these private placement offerings. Congress has required that the SEC change those rules to allow companies and promoters to offer securities directly to accredited investors through means such as direct mail, cold calls, seminars and general advertisements.

If you visit a lot of different investment websites, do not be surprised if ads for private placements start to popup in your email. The new rules permitting the direct solicitation of private placement investors are an invitation to fraudsters and scam artists. Accredited investors *will* be targeted. Make sure you know what you need to know—or invest in something else.

The SEC has just approved a new rule, Reg. A+, which will allow companies to raise up to $50 million from investors. Reg. A+ offerings will be open to all investors, not just accredited investors.

Both private placements and Reg. A+ offerings represent legitimate ways for smaller businesses to access the capital markets.

In every case, the written materials that you are given should provide you with all of the material facts and all of the pertinent documents and contracts concerning the offering and the underlying investment. The SEC is clear that its rules prohibiting fraud apply to these smaller offerings. Do not expect the SEC to back that up with enforcement actions.

Investors will really need to be careful.

If you purchase a private placement you will sign a document that says you conducted your own "due diligence" or at least that you were given the opportunity to do so. Will it be true?

Are you capable of reading and understanding the contracts that you will be asked to sign in order to buy a private placement? Do you really understand the nuances of purchasing "interests" instead of "shares"?

If you are unable to read and understand the transaction documents, then you probably will not be able to understand everything that is included in the PPM. You are certainly not going to spot what is missing.

You are buying a "pig-in-a-poke," meaning you do not really know what you are getting for your money. You should either hire someone who can evaluate the investment on your behalf or invest in something that you do understand.

If you are still considering investing in a private placement offering, here are some things that you should always consider and some questions that I think that you should ask.

1) This is a speculative investment. You are likely risking all of the money that you are investing. Can you afford to lose this money? If the honest answer is no, you would not be comfortable losing this money, ***pass.*** Similar investments with a much lower risk are frequently available in the public securities markets at a much lower commission cost.

2) Illiquid means highest risk. Unlike a stock or bond traded on an exchange or NASDAQ that you can sell at any time, securities that are issued through private placements can often not be sold. Illiquidity means that once you make this investment you should be prepared to hold it for a very long time.

If the company does well for ten years and then goes under you can still lose all of your original investment. If you will need these funds in a few years' time for other purposes, private placements may not be for you.

3) The specific risk factors associated with any private placement investment should be clearly set out for you in the PPM. You may be presented with pages and pages of "risk factors" when you purchase a private placement. They are there for a reason. If you cannot understand the risks involved with the investment or are not willing to accept them, do not invest.

If a salesperson suggests to you that these risk disclosures are "just boilerplate" or something similar, ***walk away.***

4) The people who are behind the investment are your most important consideration. They are the ones who are responsible for taking your money and the money of other investors and making more money. The PPM should tell you about their education, experience and job skills.

Be wary of disclosures about bankruptcies, felonies, regulatory actions and litigation alleging fraud involving a person who is soliciting your investment. You can invest your money with people who have not had these problems.

5) Promises of higher returns are standard. Private placements have higher risks than many other investments. Consequently, you have a right to expect a higher return than you might receive with other mainstream investments.

Evaluating the risks versus the potential for a return is the process by which you make your decision to invest or not. That process requires that you have all of the facts about the investment and that you have those facts in the proper context.

6) Pretty pictures and glossy brochures add nothing to the transaction. You are not buying a car; you are making a long-term investment. If the verified facts and financial information about the investment do not convince you, do not invest.

7) Private placements typically pay the brokerage firms and individual brokers much higher commissions than other investments. That creates conflicts that do not favor investors.

8) Internal costs are frequently high. Total up the commissions, fees and other offering costs. That is the cost to the company to acquire the funds in this offering. These costs are being paid out of the funds that are being invested. The underlying investment that you are buying must increase in value by this much for investors to break even.

9) No auditors. Many private placement companies (unlike Reg. A+ offerings) do not present audited financial information either before or after you invest. This can always be a problem. Without an audit, you are being asked to make your investment not knowing if the financial information you are considering is accurate. After you invest, you will not be able to determine how your money actually got spent.

10) No insurance. If one of the executives running this company does something inappropriate with the money that you invest or just steals it, do you have recourse? Many of these privately funded companies do not have the proper insurance to cover unanticipated loss of investor funds or errors or omissions by management.

11) The PPM will also disclose what will happen to the money that you invest. Watch out for broad categories like: *product development* or *working capital*. Investors are entitled to greater specificity as regards the use of their funds if they ask.

12) Insiders can win even if you do not. Once funded, insiders may draw high salaries or receive other fees even as the company struggles. The company may be renting space in a building or contracting work to a company owned by an insider.

13) Many private placement offerings include *financial projections* of future operations, revenues and profits. No one can predict the future and projections attempt to do just that.

The company could not raise a lot of money if it provided projections that showed that the company could not be profitable. There should be a reasonable basis for the belief that sales and cash flow can reach the levels projected.

14) Is there enough money to succeed? Companies with unproven products or technologies may run out of money before they bring the product to market. Companies still in their startup or developmental stage nonetheless have budgets, timelines and schedules.

If you are investing in a new business with a "great idea," remember that getting the idea to market takes people with business acumen and may require more money. Even an established business would want to have adequate reserves.

15) What is the exit strategy? How and when will investors get paid? Is the company counting on a public offering at a later date? Will the company or its' assets eventually be sold and the proceeds distributed to investors? How are external events likely to affect the company's prospects and timetable?

16) What happens if...? How is the company prepared to deal with potential problems? If the company succeeds, will there be enough funds to keep it going if there is a problem down the road?

17) Taxes. Many private placements are structured to comply with, and take advantage of, certain sections of the Internal Revenue Code that will provide specific tax benefits to investors. You should check with your personal accountant before you make any investment to see if the tax benefits are available and beneficial to you. You should know that if the investment is structured incorrectly, the IRS might deny those tax benefits, years after you have taken them. That can be very expensive.

18) A good idea may not succeed. Does the business plan suggest that the company can get the product to market and return a profit in a reasonable amount of time? Does the company have the resources to develop its product and follow its plan? Is the product still on the drawing board or getting ready for market? Have materials and production facilities been sourced and priced? Is there a prototype that you can inspect?

19) Who are the other investors? Are other investors active in the company's affairs or passive, like you? Are they available to provide marketing assistance or additional financing?

20) How will the company market its product? Business people, especially those trying to build a new business, can be myopic. If the business plan says that the company will sell 100,000 units per month, the company should have an adequate marketing plan to reach those customers. Beware of companies that say: *if we build it, customers will come.* Some companies put all their money into product development and have little left over for a real marketing campaign.

21) What does the company own? Who owns the assets, like buildings and equipment that are important for the company's success? Has the company patented its process? Is that great logo that appears on the company's stationery trademarked?

22) Beware of secrecy. Private placements, especially for startups, frequently require investors to agree not to disclose proprietary information about the company to anyone. That should not include your attorneys, accountants or third parties who you hire to help you evaluate the investment. If the company says that it has a process that will do great things, but it cannot or will not show you the details of how it works, be very suspicious.

23) With a private placement, stockbrokerage firms are required to conduct a reasonable investigation of the offering, the company and the people behind it. Their investigation should ***verify*** that any written materials about the offering are accurate, complete and not misleading. This is called a "due diligence investigation. "You can ask your stockbroker for details of the firm's investigation of the company. A stockbrokerage firm may be willing to share what it knows of the investment or it may not.

24) You may have recourse if a registered representative sells a private placement to you and fails to give you all of the facts, fails to conduct a reasonable due diligence investigation or if you were not a high-risk investor in the first place.

If most of the items on the above list were not already obvious to you, I would tell you that a private placement investment is probably not appropriate for you.

Over the years people have suggested to me that it may be better for most people to invest in areas about which they already know quite a bit. I would not disagree.

Many people believe that they know quite a bit about investing in gold. Gold is an investment that transcends markets and cultures. If a sack of gold coins in your safe deposit box helps you sleep at night, by all means, suit yourself. But there are other ways to own gold and the scammers are always waiting.

CHAPTER XI
Retirees in the Commodity Markets

It may seem surprising to consider that retirees lose substantial amounts of money in the commodity markets. Just about everyone understands that commodity trading is a speculative activity.

I have known a few retirees who like the action they get in the commodity markets and view their trading as recreation, like gambling in a casino. Notwithstanding, most retirees would not seem to want to take the risk with a substantial amount of their funds. When I come across a retiree with a six-figure commodity loss, I am always suspicious.

A lot of people called me for a while about a company that I will call **Mambo Financial** (not its real name). It may still be in operation.

Mambo had positioned itself as a dealer in gold bars and gold coins. If you typed the word ***gold*** into a search engine or visited a site that offered gold prices, Mambo's ad would popup.

People buy gold for a variety of reasons. Like any investment, people buy gold when they believe the price of gold will go up. Anyone contacting Mambo was predisposed to the sales pitch to buy more.

Mambo deals in what the commodity markets call *physicals*. Mambo is selling actual gold bars. You pay for the bars and they ship them to you.

If you wish, Mambo will store any gold that you buy from them for you in their vaults. There is a monthly fee, of course, for storage and insurance. Mambo Financial also offered a gold trading scheme that was quite unique.

If you call Mambo to buy a few gold bars, the salesperson will tell you about the great success he and his clients have had with their trading program.

The pitch: *You called to buy gold at today's price because you thought it would be more expensive down the road. The program helps you to make more money when the price does move up.*

If you buy some gold bars from Mambo for cash and leave them in their vault as collateral, Mambo will loan you the money to buy more gold and will hold it all as collateral for the loan. If gold goes up a few dollars an ounce, you would make more money because you would own more ounces of gold. After a while you would sell and then settle up with Mambo.

This functioned exactly like a margin account would function at a stockbrokerage firm. Margin accounts at stockbrokerage firms are regulated by the SEC and by the Federal Reserve.

A stockbrokerage firm cannot loan money to a customer on margin unless the collateral is in place. A commodity futures contract, such as would be traded on a commodity futures exchange, uses leverage differently and is subject to different regulations.

Mambo's program mimicked a standard margin account but was backed by gold bars, not stocks. Like a margin account the leverage increased the investors' potential for profit, at the same time it increased the risk of loss.

Using round numbers, let us say that the price of gold is $1000 per ounce. I have $30,000 and wish to buy thirty ounces. If the price of gold goes up ten dollars to $1010 per ounce, I will make $300 minus the cost of storage and insurance.

Under Mambo's program, I can use my 30 bars as a down payment on a purchase of up to four times as many bars as I own, in this case another 120 bars. Mambo will let me buy 150 bars for the same $30,000 and if the price of gold goes up to $1010, I will make $1500.

I will be paying more for monthly storage and insurance because I am storing 150 ounces of gold. I am also now paying interest on a loan with a face amount of $120,000.

After a month or two the interest and fees start to add up and I will owe more. If the price of gold takes a dip, the gold Mambo is holding as collateral will be worth less and Mambo will ask me to make margin calls. I either add more money or cash out and take the loss.

Mambo salesmen would counsel: *Okay, you lost last month. Put up another $20,000 and try again because now that the price of gold has come down from last month the price is sure to go up.*

Mambo made its money on the margin interest and storage and other fees and had a slick bookkeeping system that showed people how many ounces of gold that they had in storage, what it was worth and what their loan balance was every day.

In a great many cases, people would not want to add more money to meet the margin calls and the gold that the customers had purchased would come back to Mambo. Mambo returned to the customers only the amount that the trade would have left them, pocketing the rest. Once they had repossessed the gold each time, Mambo could sell it again.

It sounds simple and legitimate until you ask the questions: *Was there actually gold in the vault or were all of the transactions just bookkeeping entries? Was there enough gold if everyone who had purchased gold had paid off their loans and had taken delivery?*

In all probability Mambo was **bucketing**—taking real orders and confirming them to customers but not actually having the gold to sell or ever intending to buy gold with the customers' money. Mambo was just making book.

An honest bookie changes the odds to keep the amount of offsetting bets equal. Mambo stacked the deck with interest and fees so that the customers would lose money. Bucketing is illegal in almost every state—but maybe not for Mambo.

The commodity markets in the US provide a different function than the capital markets and are subject to different regulations and oversight. Commodity regulations focus on the organized commodity contract and futures exchanges and provide little regulation to the physical markets.

Mambo has built a business model based upon the physical delivery of the gold from Mambo to its customers and back again. I can say that because the account agreements and other paperwork that the customers sign in order to do business with Mambo made it clear how the program was supposed to work.

In reality, the gold never left the vault. Mambo had structured its program so that it was neither a security nor a regulated commodity contract. Because it was neither, there were no federal regulations prohibiting Mambo from doing its business as it wished.

Customers were angry with Mambo because they had been considering buying gold as a safe place to store money. They came away with no gold and less money and a feeling that they had been swindled.

Although originally seen in stock cases, bucketing seems more common as of late with commodity firms. Many commodity firms and advisors are unregulated. Few are as sophisticated as Mambo.

I know of one group from Hong Kong that came to San Francisco, set up shop and fleeced a few hundred people out of a few million dollars bucketing commodity trades.

The people behind the scam were of a specific Asian ethnicity and dealt primarily with members of that community in the Bay Area. Their trading room was noisy like a casino. "Traders" were screaming into telephones, seemingly trading gold and other precious metals in world markets. All of it was fake.

The group then pulled up stakes and repeated the same scam in Miami before they were caught and prosecuted. The money had been long sent to Hong Kong and from there the customers' money disappeared into the untraceable world banking system.

If you want to gamble in the commodity markets, then you can buy and sell contracts, futures and options through firms that are members of the organized and regulated commodity exchanges. Once you start to deal with people on the periphery of these markets, you are asking to be scammed.

My personal favorite commodity scam is the **computerized commodity trading system**. If you fall for this one, you are going to have to take at least some of the responsibility.

If you do trade commodities, then you know that it is very risky and that many people who try to trade commodities lose their money. You also know that each trade is leveraged, which increases your risk at the same time that it is increases your chance for profit.

Commodity traders typically use what is called *technical trading analysis.* Technical analysis estimates prices based upon supply and demand for each particular commodity that is trading in the organized markets. Traders use a process called *charting,* trying to predict how the price of the commodities they are following will perform. Commodity traders have been charting for decades. Since charting is essentially a mathematical process, it is easy to see why computers would be logical tools to assign to it.

Commodity markets are interrelated, both across time zones and across markets. The price of one commodity may be affected by the price of other commodities as traders move out of one and into another. Commodity prices can be influenced by fluctuations in currency values and a plethora of other factors including weather and politics across broad, global markets.

Imagine if you could get a computer program that would analyze all of this data about the various commodity markets, in real time, and then *correctly* tell you what and when to buy and sell. This scam seems to appeal to engineers and others who have logical minds and who believe that numbers can validate anything.

The sales pitch for these computer programs usually includes claims of *verifiable results* showing the profitable trading results of an account utilizing the program. Even if true, the results would be meaningless. What happened in the markets yesterday is not an indication of what will happen tomorrow.

The hype is always for the newest software. These do not have years of actual trading results that can be verified because they are brand new. Instead, the programmers will tell you that they ***back-tested*** the program to determine what it would have done in real world situations and came away with superior results and profits. If the test results said otherwise, you would never see them.

If a computer program could successfully trade in the commodity markets, then it would be able to do so continually over a significant number of years. If any of these programs could consistently place winning trades across the commodity markets as they claim to be able to do, then be assured that Goldman Sacks and JP Morgan would have outbid each other for the software long ago.

I have spoken with too many very intelligent people who laid out thousands of dollars for these programs and thousands more for hookups and commissions for something that did not, and could not have worked.

There is no such thing as a computer program that can accurately predict the commodities markets, or any other markets, for that matter. There is no person or group, computer-aided or otherwise that can accurately predict future commodity prices repeatedly and over the long term. Do not buy into any one who claims that they can.

Trading, whether of commodities, options or stocks, is a strategy that holds positions for a very short time, sometimes hours or days. Traders are looking for short-term profits from small movements in the price of shares.

Where an investor might hold shares for a year hoping the share price might go up $20; a trader might buy and sell the same shares when they are up $2 per share hoping to replicate that result, trade after trade throughout the year.

You would not buy commodities for the long-term in any event. Commodity contracts expire. When they do the owner of the contract will be entitled to take delivery of some number of railroad cars full of the commodity in question, such as corn or wheat or hogs. If you are not a farmer or an end user (like a corn chip snack manufacturer) you are a trader. In order to make money, professional traders usually trade every day. Commission costs are always a concern for any trader.

Retirees and many others are sometimes counseled to include **managed futures** funds in their portfolios. Managed futures funds operate like mutual funds. They pool investors' money and use it to trade commodity contracts, futures and options on a large scale. Like mutual funds, no two are exactly alike. How well the fund performs is usually left to a professional trader. Past performance, as you know, is not an indicator that you will make money.

Managed futures are often recommended to retirees to put a little *oomph* in their portfolio. A managed futures fund, because it is leveraged and because the futures market can be volatile, can produce larger gains and potentially greater losses than the stock market.

People are sometimes told that managed futures can ***hedge or offset other portfolio risks***. That is usually not true. In general terms, you cannot reduce the risk of a portfolio by adding more risky investments to it.

Trading commodity futures contracts is always speculative. If an advisor suggests that you invest a small amount, say 5% of your portfolio into a managed futures fund for whatever reason, you should be prepared to kiss that money goodbye. It may work out in your favor, but do not invest in anything that has to do with commodities or futures unless you are using money that you are prepared to lose.

The commodity trading advisors who run these funds necessarily make a lot of trades earning lots and lots of commissions for the firms at which they trade. Many of the larger stockbrokerage firms also belong to the commodity exchanges and can capture that commission by handling the trades for the funds that they recommend. Stockbrokers and investment advisors who sell these funds get a commission as well.

It should not be difficult for you to see that, by suggesting that many portfolios should have 5% of their value invested in managed futures funds, a firm might divert substantial sums into a risky product where the investors' money will be churned through a lot of trades, earning substantial commissions for the firm every day. This arrangement where *"we only offer funds that trade with us"* is an obvious conflict of interest that is nonetheless commonplace.

Who is watching out for you? Only you and no one else.

CHAPTER XII
Investing with an Insurance Company

Millions of people own billions of dollars worth of annuity contracts using funds that are specifically earmarked for retirement. People buy annuities when they are young and allow their funds to grow according to the policy terms or add to it as they go along.

One of the primary advantages of annuities is the tax-deferred buildup of income inside of the annuity. Annuities are not taxed until withdrawals are taken from the account, allowing the owner to compound their earnings tax-free. IRA accounts do much the same and almost always charge less in fees.

With a basic **fixed annuity** the insurance company will pay you interest during the accumulation period and will pay you the lump sum that has accumulated when you retire.

If you wish, the company will make payments to you over a number of years instead. The interest rate that the insurance company will pay during the accumulation period may differ from the rate it will pay during the distribution period. People who buy annuities like the fact that they can calculate now exactly how much of a check they will receive years later.

Annuities will generally pay higher interest to you than a bank would. An annuity payment for a deferred annuity contract (usually ten or twenty years) will always be part interest, part return of your own principal.

If you put your money into a savings account at a bank, you know that the savings account is insured by the FDIC. Since the account is insured by an agency of the US Government, regulations allow the bank to represent that the account is "safe" and "insured by the FDIC."

Annuities are backed only by the insurance companies that write them. They are the only investment that is permitted to use the word "guaranteed" in their advertising.

The success or failure of an annuity is dependent upon the ability of the insurance company to make the payments that it is promising to make. Month in and month out, most insurance companies do honor their annuity contract commitments. You should still investigate and consider the financial strength of any insurance company that will be holding onto your money for twenty or thirty years. You should also know that insurance companies that will pay a little more to get your money might not be as creditworthy as a company that pays a little less.

In the mid-1990s, the insurance industry introduced the **equity-indexed annuity** as a variation of the traditional, fixed-interest, deferred annuity contract. The stock market was hot at the time and investors were not happy with the lower returns that fixed annuities paid, even if the return was stable.

An indexed annuity ties the performance of the account not to a fixed rate of interest but to the performance of a stock market index such as the Standard & Poor's 500. The insurance company is not investing in the stocks that are in the index; they are agreeing that if the index goes up, they will pay you more.

If you purchase an equity-indexed annuity for a fixed period of time you will usually earn a guaranteed minimum rate of interest. If the stock market index to which the annuity is pegged goes up then the company will pay you a portion of that gain as well. Again, the insurance company may or may not be investing in stocks; they are just promising to pay you more if stocks go up.

Your extra payment might be subject to a *cap rate* that will limit you to a maximum payout even if the index does better. Your payout might be limited to a portion of the increase in the index, what is known as a *participation rate*. Exactly how the insurance company will calculate your additional payments and when they will pay you will vary company-to-company and contract-to-contract.

The sales pitch for indexed annuities offers investors the ability to obtain a return based upon stock market gains in years that the market goes up without any penalty or loss of principal in years that the market goes down. You will get a ***higher return*** when stock market goes up, a ***guaranteed minimum rate*** if the market goes down and you will ***never lose money***. Sound good?

The insurance industry has dressed these indexed annuities up with slick brochures and fancy charts and graphs; ***the promise of upside potential without risk of loss*** and pays thousands of sales people very high commissions to sell them.

These annuities do have the benefits of tax deferral. At the same time, if you wish to tie your retirement account to the stock market, there are mutual funds and ETFs that will accomplish much of the same purpose for much less cost. Index annuities are expensive and often contain multiple layers of fees that may not be evident or clearly disclosed.

Index annuities are intended to be long-term investments—usually ten to fifteen years. It can take years before the commissions and front-end fees are recouped. That is why they are often considered by younger or middle-aged investors. Selling investments that take a long time to break even to senior citizens is always a problem.

The real bad boys of annuity contracts, at least as far as seniors and retirees are concerned, are ***variable annuities***. Selling variable annuities to seniors is widespread and is a serious problem. **There is probably more written by regulators about what is wrong with selling variable annuities to senior citizens than any other financial product that I will mention in this book.** At the same time, variable annuity sales to seniors are growing every year.

With a variable annuity, the insurance company does not adjust your annuity payments in line with a stock market index. With a variable annuity you will actually invest your money in the markets and your funds are at normal market risk.

The insurance company may offer a range of investment options. The investment options for a variable annuity are typically mutual funds that invest in stocks, bonds, money market instruments or some combination of the three.

The value of your investment as a variable annuity owner will vary depending on the performance of the investment options that you choose.

If your intention is to allocate and rebalance your portfolio within the annuity, you should understand that it will be difficult to do so properly. The funds will not correlate well with each other and may not offset each other in such a way as to substantially reduce market risks.

The insurance company will sell you various guarantees, which will provide for a minimum return every year even if the market goes down. You will pay for every rider and option that you select.

A common feature of variable annuities is the death benefit. If you die, a person you select as a beneficiary (such as your spouse or child) will receive the greater of: (i) all the money in your account, or (ii) some guaranteed minimum (such as all purchase payments minus prior withdrawals). Other features may include long-term care insurance, which pays for home health care or nursing home care if you become seriously ill.

Most variable annuity contracts include an annual mortality and expense (M&E) fee. This charge is equal to a certain percentage of your account value, typically in the range of 1.25% per year. This charge compensates the insurance company for insurance risks it assumes under the annuity contract.

Profit from the mortality and expense risk charge is sometimes used to pay the insurer's costs of selling the variable annuity, such as a commission paid to your financial professional for selling the variable annuity to you. The company may include the fees for any guarantees that you buy or may charge you separately for them.

You will also pay a management fee for each mutual fund. As with all mutual funds, fees will reduce returns. The "expense ratio" of each fund should be disclosed to you.

You should add up all of the annual fees. Over ten or twenty years those fees can add up to a substantial amount of money. Your portfolio will need to earn that much more than the market every year for you to match the market's performance.

Variable annuities are long-term investments and if you purchase one, you should do so while you are still years away from retirement. Between the high commissions and significant initial fees it can take a long time to recoup your costs just to break even. That is why selling a variable annuity to someone who is already in their 60s raises the eyebrows on many people, including insurance and securities regulators, consumer organizations and lawyers like me.

Variable annuities are the only kind of annuity that requires the salesperson to have both an insurance license and a securities registration. They are often complicated. The salesperson with whom you speak will only be able to sell you an annuity contract issued by one of the few companies with whom they are licensed. If you want to "shop around" for an annuity, I would recommend that you look at quite a few. No two annuity contracts are exactly alike.

A variable annuity sale will pay the salesperson who is pitching one to you a very high commission—higher than the commission on almost any other financial product. The commission on a variable annuity contract may be 7% or 10% or more of the amount that you invest.

If you buy a million dollar policy, the salesperson who sells it to you may earn a commission of $70,000 or more. You can see why some people who sell investments really like to sell variable annuities.

If you withdraw money from a variable annuity within a certain period after a purchase payment (typically within six to eight years, but sometimes as long as ten years), the insurance company usually will assess a "surrender" charge, which is a type of sales charge.

Generally, the surrender charge is a percentage of the amount withdrawn, and declines gradually over a period of several years, known as the "surrender period." For example, a 7% charge might apply in the first year after a purchase payment, 6% in the second year, 5% in the third year, and so on until the eighth year, when the surrender charge no longer applies.

Often, contracts will allow you to withdraw part of your account value each year—10% or 15% of your account value, for example— without paying a surrender charge. The rule of thumb is that the first years' surrender charge is equal to the commission that the company paid a salesperson to sell the annuity to you.

Whatever type of annuity you buy you can take out a lump sum at the end of the accumulation period or you can take periodic distributions. Typically, the distributions will last for a fixed period of time—ten or twenty years. What you will get back during that period is your own money plus what it has earned minus what you took out, lost or which has already been distributed to you.

If you retire at age 65 and take your payments over twenty years, then at the end of the contract your payments will stop. People are living longer. What happens if you celebrate your 85th birthday and will still have bills to pay next month and the month after? Your twenty-year annuity will seem shortsighted.

The fear of running out of money before they die keeps baby boomers up at night. With an annuity you can arrange for the insurance company to send you a check for as long as you live.

The *get a check every month for as long as you live* sales pitch is very tempting to retirees. You can purchase an annuity that will make payments to you for the rest of your life or for the life of your surviving spouse, but these options are not free.

Let me ask it another way. How much would you be willing to pay today for a check in the amount of $1000 per month for as long as you live? Certainly, your age, health and family history of longevity will be factors in computing your answer.

An insurance company will ask you about those same things when it is trying to assess its risk of promising to give you a check every month for as long as you live. The insurance company is better at these calculations than you are and the insurance industry as a whole finds these *check until you die* provisions very profitable.

A variable annuity will not pay you a check *every month for as long as you live* and then pay you back the rest of your money if any is left. From the company's perspective, you pay a lump sum premium in return for which the company promises to send you a check for a specified amount every month until you die.

When you die, the payments stop and whatever amount of your money that might have been left now belongs to the company. Annuities are often favored by people who do not want a relative or charity to inherit their money.

If you do the math, you will see why the *check for as long as you live* option may not be as good as it sounds, unless you are the insurance company.

As a baseline number, if you have $1 million at retirement and purchase bonds or dividend-paying stocks paying a rate of 6%, your monthly check will be $5000. After twenty years or whenever the bonds mature, you still have your principal. As long as you do not invade your principal, you will not run out of money.

If you convert a previously purchased annuity to a twenty-year fixed annuity at age 65, and it pays you an interest rate of 6%, your monthly check will be closer to $7200. The difference is that the annuity payment is intentionally invading your principal every month and paying part of it back to you. At the end of twenty years you will have nothing left. If you die before the twenty years are up, the payments are still made to your beneficiaries.

Many people are drawn to the "check a month until you die option." The customers are thinking that they might live into their 90s or beyond. They do not want to run out of money, especially at that advanced age. The insurance company knows that its customers might be thinking (encouraged by the salespeople) that they may live that long.

The math for the "check a month until you die" option is stacked in the insurance company's favor. The average age at death of the pool of thousands of annuity customers will likely be in the mid-70s.

Many of the customers in the pool will die before the insurance company has paid out to them as much as they put in. If you want to get out more than you paid in, you will have to live for a good long time.

The fact is that most people who live to age 65 will not live to see their 85th birthday. The insurance industry will always tell you to plan as if you will.

I have seen studies that suggest that as many as one in five retirees are being sold some type of annuity. It should be obvious that in many cases much of what annuities promise can be accomplished with simpler, less expensive products and strategies.

Variable annuities have a very high risk of loss and pay among the highest commissions that the salesperson can earn. Billions of dollars' worth of variable annuities are sold every year to retirees and seniors for whom these products are really not suitable.

If you do not think that there is a direct correlation between those two facts you have not been paying attention.

CHAPTER XIII

The Smartest People in the Business

I do not know whether it is ego or hubris but many people who are entrusted to invest large sums of other people's money do some very stupid things.

One of the firms that I will discuss, BBC and Co., is really a top international investment bank. I wanted to show you what actually occurs at the top of the money management ladder.

I represented a very nice couple in their late 40s, whom I will call Mr. and Mrs. Jones. Mr. Jones was an engineer who had been working his way up in the same industry for twenty years. With the help of some stock options at two different companies along the way, and by swapping their home in Silicon Valley in which they had lived for more than a decade for one outside Boston, they found themselves with about $5 million in cash.

Mr. Jones asked the CFO of his company for a referral and found himself meeting with Joe Smith (not his real name), a professional money manager who worked for the Wealth Management Division of one of the large, old school investment banks, **BBC and Co**. (not its real name, either).

BBC is very much part of the establishment in every financial market in the world. Not everyone in the financial services industry can work for a top-of-the-line firm like BBC, which Mr. Smith had done for almost thirty years.

At the time that he first met Mr. and Mrs. Jones, Mr. Smith was managing about $300 million for some of the bank's wealthy clients. Surely the bank would not let Mr. Smith manage other peoples' money if he did not know what he was doing?

All went along pretty well for a while until Mr. Smith decided to make what is known as an *interest rate bet*. An interest rate bet is the same transaction that drove Orange County, California into bankruptcy in 1994. In that case the bet was that interest rates would go lower and stay lower but the thought process was very much the same.

The Orange County Treasurer had been managing several billions of dollars in county funds and pension money for county employees for more than twenty years. Over those years he had generally been able to obtain better results than other similar state funds. This return was attributed to his good advisors at Merrill Lynch.

Sometime in 1994, those good advisors suggested to the Treasurer that, using *derivatives*, he should take a $20 billion bet that interest rates would go down, even though he was managing only about $7 billion at the time. The leverage and the extra-sized bet were intended to make extra-sized profits when interest rates declined, which the Treasurer and his Merrill Lynch advisors were certain that interest rates would do.

The markets, of course, did just the opposite causing the county to lose about $1.6 billion of its $7 billion fund. The county filed for bankruptcy protection because it could not pay its bondholders and its pension obligations. The bankruptcy roiled the municipal bond markets and the credit markets in general and actually caused interest rates to rise all by themselves.

In his defense the Orange County Treasurer argued that he had been misled by Merrill Lynch and specifically by the Merrill Lynch executives with whom he had dealt. The way things worked out was not the way in which they had drawn it up, he argued; no one had ever suggested that the County could lose that much money.

In response to his *I only did what Merrill Lynch told me to do* defense, Merrill Lynch offered that the Treasurer was a very sophisticated money manager in his own right and understood everything that they had proposed as regards this particular strategy. Merrill told anyone who would listen that their strategy was a good one for the county, even though they were wrong about the direction of interest rates, given what the county wanted, which was higher returns.

Merrill Lynch ultimately settled all the claims against it for about 25 cents on a dollar. Merrill walked away with the commissions, fees and markups for the securities that it did sell to Orange County and in the end, those fees were quite sizeable. I bring this up because many financial professionals never learned the lessons of the Orange County debacle. That included Mr. Smith.

In response to the financial crisis in 2008, the US government began a policy to keep interest rates very low. Mr. Smith and many other people never liked this policy. By 2011, Mr. Smith believed that the government would begin to let interest rates rise and set out to profit from his beliefs.

Mr. Smith placed his bet by *shorting STRIPS* with almost all of the funds across all of the accounts that he managed—a total of about $250 million. He actually sold off other investments in his customers' accounts to have cash with which to place his bet.

STRIPS are a *derivative* of US Treasury securities. Because they are derivatives and not US Treasuries themselves and because they are leveraged, STRIPS are more volatile than many other interest-rate sensitive securities.

The government did not raise interest rates—as Mr. Smith believed that they would—and actually continued to lower them. The trades in the STRIPS that Mr. Smith had made for his customers, including Mr. and Mrs. Jones, lost about 40% of their value before they were closed out several months later.

All together, Mr. Smith's customers lost about $100 million ($250 million x 40%) and Mr. and Mrs. Jones lost $2 million of the $5 million that they had entrusted to the Mr. Smith and to the bank for *professional* wealth management.

No one contests that Mr. Smith had the legal right to make the trades that he made. The written management contract gave him full discretion to manage the account as he saw fit. Any restrictions that might have been imposed by any regulation that was intended to limit his actions were set aside by the paperwork.

The bank itself had a stable full of economists and research analysts in various world banking centers who spent their time analyzing the direction of interest rates. The bank itself was arguably very close to the epicenter of interest rate decisions worldwide.

At the arbitration hearing on this claim, I asked Mr. Smith: *Wasn't it true if the bank wanted to know what the US government was going to do about interest rates, the President of the bank could just call the Secretary of the Treasury and ask?*

Mr. Smith had decided not to use all of the substantial resources of the bank when he was developing the strategy that he was to use for his customers. I highlight this because most people do not realize that when they hire an investment advisor they are not necessarily hiring the institution at which the advisor works in any meaningful way.

Mr. Smith had access to all of the vast resources of the bank. He chose to use his own judgment to focus his attention on *some* of the information that the bank had available.

I believe that Mr. Smith used the data that he compiled to support his predetermined belief that the government policy had been wrong all along and that it had certainly outlived its usefulness. He had the data that said to him that the government *should* have raised interest rates and he placed his bet accordingly.

Governments do not always act as rational economists think that they should. The US government kept interest rates low. At the same time, the bank's own economists had predicted that rates would stay low and the bank was investing its own money and making loans based upon that belief.

I am not suggesting that the bank should have adopted a one-shoe-fits-all approach, investing all of its managed accounts in the same way. On something as fundamental as interest rates, however, one would have to ask why Mr. Smith thought that he knew better than all of the economists and senior officials at the bank whose job it was to keep track of and specifically to forecast interest rate changes.

Frequently, a money manager who works for a large institution is not given the leeway that Mr. Smith enjoyed to render investment advice that is contrary to the advice that the high priced analysts who work for the firm are giving. Perhaps, given his longevity at the firm, Mr. Smith had some reason to believe that the reasoning of the professional analysts at the firm was flawed.

Personally, I believe that Mr. Smith came up with the strategy for an interest rate bet of this magnitude because Mr. Smith also had an extra bonus incentive. Under the terms of the management agreement with the customers, BBC and Mr. Smith were to receive a bonus equal to 20% of the profits that each account he managed earned, year over year.

This type of profit-sharing relationship between an investment advisor and a customer is common with some professional hedge fund managers. It is not the norm for most retail investors who are looking to have a few million dollars managed by a professional investment advisor.

This fee structure was clearly set out in the management contract. Mr. and Mrs. Jones had not objected to it. The bonus was touted as an extra incentive for Mr. Smith to do really well for his clients.

We know that Mr. Smith placed his bet in the aggregate amount of approximately $250 million and lost 40% or $100 million across all of the accounts that he managed. What if he had won the bet?

Had the government cooperated and things gone Mr. Smith's way, Mr. and Mrs. Jones, who lost about 40% of the $5 million they had on the table might have won an equal amount, approximately $2 million. The rest of Mr. Smith's customers would have had a similar result.

Mr. Smith and BBC would have contractually been entitled to receive 20% of the winnings, which would have aggregated to $20 million to be shared between them ($250 million x 40% profit x 20% incentive fee). At the arbitration hearing, I suggested that had this occurred, it would have been a *retirement event* for Mr. Smith who had already worked at the bank for 30 years. What would you call it?

These types of conflicts are rampant in the financial services industry and especially in the wealth management side of the business. The contracts that you sign with any large financial institution are not going to be in your favor.

There is no reason to believe that you cannot obtain competent and professional investment advice from an advisor not affiliated with a large institution. The larger the firm, the more they necessarily care about their procedures and their profitability. That profitability comes from your account and the accounts of other customers.

More and more, I hear that the best money managers work for private hedge funds. I do not believe that to be true either. I have represented more than one client in a hedge fund whose manager did something stupid. Very few hedge fund managers seem to be worth a 20% bonus for doing their jobs.

If one investment advisory firm was truly better than all of the others and truly made the most money for its clients' year in and year out, it would be no secret. The investment committee of every retirement and pension fund (and every charity and endowment) would direct their funds to that firm and that would be that.

One independent advisory firm in particular spends a substantial amount of money marketing its brand and its services. It presents itself as a successful, professional investment advisory firm. This firm will tell you that *they really understand the financial markets and the motivations of investors.*

Over the years, several people had contacted me and asked me to sue this firm because the firm had not delivered on the promises that it had made. Each of these people had substantial losses in their accounts that were being managed by this firm.

I call this firm Malarky Investments (not it's real name). It is one of the largest, most respected independent money managers around. They have tens of billions of dollars under management. They manage money for county treasurers and university endowments, large corporate pension funds and a lot of wealthy and not so wealthy people.

I also single this company out because they seem to aggressively target retirees with their advertising. If you search around the Internet looking for information about investments for retirees, this firm will likely come up because they spend a lot of money advertising to that market.

They offer a booklet with a title something like: *101 Reasons Why Retirees Should Hire Us to Invest Their Money*. If you send them an email to request the booklet, ads for this company will pop up in your email for a long time.

The owner of the company, Mr. Malarky (not his real name) has built an immensely successful investment advisory business that is the envy of his industry because he is an excellent salesman. Malarkey Investments sells the idea that *it can make money for its clients every year*. The firm has the proper disclaimers in its written materials but sit in on a sales meeting aimed at a sizeable account and all you will hear is: *success, success, success*.

For the record, rarely does an investment advisor investing in a broad portfolio of stocks make money every year; ten years in a row would be a unique accomplishment.

Malarky claims that it has been investing its clients' money profitably for each of the last fifteen years. The company claims to have gotten its clients out of tech stocks before the tech stock market crashed in 2000-2001 and into *defensive stocks* in early 2008 so that its customers maintained their profits when the market crashed again.

Malarky Investments also promises every client a *personalized portfolio*. Every customer gets their own separate account and their own holdings but there is nothing personalized about it.

Rather, Malarky operates as if it were investing for a large mutual fund. Instead of shares in a mutual fund, each customer gets shares of the individual companies that the firm is buying for all of its customers. Every customer's account basically mirrors every other customer's account.

Given the tens of billions of dollars that it manages, Malarky Investments is actually a small operation with just a few analysts on staff. That, in and of itself, is not the problem. It does limit the number of investments that can be analyzed and followed. Malarky explains this by asserting that it only needs to follow a small group of stocks because it *screens out* the rest.

Malarky will tell you that they have *developed proprietary algorithms* which eliminate more than 95% of stocks that they could buy and then re-sort and re-analyze the 5% that are left, selecting only those that they believe to be the best-of-the-best for their clients.

Malarky's algorithms apparently include both fundamental and technical analysis so they get the right stocks at the right price. It certainly sounds good.

Allow me to translate. Unlike the commodity software, which was predicting small swings in broad markets, Malarky is using software to analyze the balance sheets of individual companies and also the trading patterns of their stocks. Many investment advisors use something similar, if not as sophisticated as the system that Malarky claims to use. In every case, the results are hit or miss.

The entire purpose of this exercise is to identify stocks whose prices will go up. Malarky says that their system works, and has worked consistently for fifteen years, in good markets and bad ones. A computer program that consistently identifies stocks whose prices will go up? Certainly they can back that up with *audited* results, right?

Given how many county treasurers, universities, charities and pension committees presumably vetted Malarky Investments, how could they have missed the fact that Malarky never had an auditor *verify* its claims of investment success?

I should not have to remind these fiduciary investors that Bernie Madoff made similar claims of year-in and year-out investment success. His results were not audited by a reputable accounting firm, either.

Malarky's excuse: *Our clients know how well their portfolios have done. Their actual trading records are private and proprietary information. Malarky's past performance is no guarantee of the results that customers may obtain in the future in any event.*

Up in the sales department *all* they are selling is Malarky's long term investment success. You would think that they would be willing to back it up.

As I said, I represented several retirees who were customers of Malarky Investments who definitely had losses in their accounts. Malarky offered three defenses.

First defense: that they cannot and do not guarantee results. My response: Fair enough, but it is contrary to the sales pitch and all of the hype.

Second defense: that these clients had not stayed long enough for results to even out. They only had paper losses when they left; if they had stayed with Malarky the portfolio would have eventually turned profitable. My response: Malarky did not expect the losses in the first place. How could they know that losses might not continue?

Third defense: these were personalized portfolios. Some customers win; others lose. My response: As I said, there was nothing personal about these portfolios; everyone basically got stocks in the same companies. Either the algorithms work or they do not.

Nothing about Malarky's methods should have been attractive to retirees in the first place. Malarky was selling the idea that it could consistently pick stocks whose prices would appreciate. If they could do it, they would not need to spend so much money advertising.

If such as system could be developed everyone would use it and everyone would want to purchase the same stocks.

The Orange County Treasurer was an experienced, knowledgeable and sophisticated investor. Merrill Lynch and BBC are two top-of-the-line, mainstream financial firms that certainly have the resources to get it right, if anyone can. Governments and very sophisticated investors call upon Malarky for advice.

Between them, they manage hundreds of billions of dollars for the largest businesses, unions, universities, charities and endowments. But their clients are a small sampling of the investors and investment committees that are looking for the "best" investment advisor.

If you give $10,000,000 to each of the twenty best investment advisors that you can find, and ask each to set up two portfolios—one for growth and one for income—you would likely get widely disparate portfolios for each type.

The value of these portfolios five or ten years down the road would likely be significantly different as well.

So how do you find the right investment advisor for you? Learn to ask the right questions.

CHAPTER XIV

How to Find a Really Good Investment Advisor

The financial services industry has changed its focus since I began working in it in the mid-1970s. At that time stockbrokers serviced their customers by researching stocks and by making recommendations that made their customers money.

I am old enough to remember when all stockbrokerage firms charged the same commission for the same transaction. Firms differentiated themselves by the advice that they gave.

Make no mistake, when your stockbroker told you to *buy* a stock it was for one reason only; the stockbroker believed that the price of the stock would go *up*. Early on someone suggested to me that stockbrokers are like lawyers; they make money because the right words come out of their mouths.

Today, more and more people seem to be comfortable with the idea of hiring an advisor to manage their investments for them on a wholly discretionary basis. The financial services industry has embraced this model for some time. The amount of *managed* funds grows year after year. "Assets under management" has become a metric for the entire industry.

If you are in the market for a new investment advisor, whether you are already retired or still working up to it, you can and should shop around and do some research. **Your search for an advisor should focus on the technical skills of the person who is actually selecting the investments that you will buy.**

The investment advisory business is huge. The competition to manage your money, between investment advisors, stockbrokers, banks, and trust and insurance companies is fierce. There are good advisors, bad advisors and mediocre ones.

It would seem obvious that everyone would want to hire the same advisor—the smartest advisor in the pack. That person does not exist. The financial services industry views the best investment advisors in the business as those who make the most money for themselves and for their firms, not for their customers.

If you go to a large financial institution, in all probability you will speak with a salesperson. They are salespeople; whatever they tell you, it is a sales pitch.

If you hire a large institution, you will probably pay more up front to set up your portfolio, as well as higher monthly fees or higher transaction fees. If the firm absorbs the transaction fees in the account, then you are probably paying markups and hidden fees on some or all of your transactions.

Managing money is a specialized profession. Money managers are expected to be more knowledgeable about investing and the financial markets than their customers. However, many professional managers do not know enough to do their jobs competently.

It is common practice in the industry that most customers interact with salespeople rather than the person who will actually manage their portfolios. Having both a salesperson and a portfolio manager or managers necessarily increases costs. Costs are always paid by the investors.

Many people are satisfied to obtain professional management at reduced costs and without commissions by investing in mutual funds directly from one of the big, no-load companies, like Vanguard or Fidelity. This is fine as long as you are comfortable without having someone to tell you when to sell or switch funds.

Personally, I am willing pay a little more for advice directed specifically to me and for personal service that comes with working with the owner of a small firm.

I believe that it is important to meet with the person who will actually invest your money and to understand how the advisor will select the investments that you will buy. I think that a smaller firm will be able to react more quickly to changes in the market if the need arises. I also believe that a smaller firm will be more accountable to me than will a larger firm if there is any kind of problem.

Advisory fees are calculated as percentage of the portfolio value so the advisors' fees grow as the portfolio grows. This incentive to make your money grow would seem to put advisors and their customers on the same page. In many cases, it does not.

Investment advisors are expected to place the needs and interests of their customers first in every instance. Any investment advisor should take care not to lose the money that is entrusted to them. Lawyers call this a *fiduciary* standard of care and conduct. Placing the financial interests of the customers above all else is a lofty goal. Not every investment advisor succeeds.

Regulations governing the conduct of investment advisors can be pretty strict, but there are loopholes. Many of the rules, regulations and safeguards that have been enacted by Congress and the SEC can be reversed if you are willing to sign away your rights.

Investment advisors are less policed than traditional stockbrokers and the industry is full of slick marketing and bad investment ideas.

You should have a *written contract* with *any* investment advisor that you hire. If you hire an advisor that is affiliated with a large, established financial institution, I should not have to tell you that the fine print in the investment advisory contract that you sign will favor them, not you.

You can find a lot of advice on the web about how to pick an investment advisor, much of it from the people who are consumer specialists. I personally believe that you should discard a lot of this advice.

I recommend that you judge an investment advisor on two scales: 1) how they will handle your portfolio and 2) how they will handle you.

Advisors will tout the record of their prior performance or how much better they performed last year than a broad market index. Whatever they may have done in the past will not affect how well they will do with the funds that you entrust to them. If you are paying for their services you have a right to expect better results than just the market average.

To distinguish themselves one from another, even the larger advisory firms will hype ridiculous statistics. For example, one large investment advisory firm uses what are called *Monte Carlo simulations* to support their financial planning for advisory customers.

A Monte Carlo simulation is a statistical analysis of possible outcomes from various long-term investment portfolios. Like all statistical analysis, a Monte Carlo simulation can only be as good as the data and assumptions upon which it is based. In most cases using a Monte Carlo analysis to predict the return of an investment portfolio is a charade.

A Monte Carlo analysis that I thought was particularly troubling was given to an older widow who was seeking investment advice after her husband had passed away. She was already drawing from the account to pay monthly bills and was clearly an income investor. There was no reason to discuss long- term growth with her in the first place.

Notwithstanding, the Monte Carlo analysis put out by this particular advisory firm as part of a fifty-page financial plan specifically told this prospective customer that with a long-term growth portfolio her "downside risk" was a 17% loss in the event of a severe market turndown. How wonderful it would be if this were true. It was not true, and in the context that it was presented to this prospective customer of an investment advisor, it was obviously misleading.

There is a reason why many investments include the disclaimer: *Past performance is no indication of future results.* The reason is: it is true. No analysis that looks at past results in the financial markets over the long-term can be accurate predicting the future.

Financial markets are evolving with technology and expanding globally at an unprecedented rate. Market statistics from as little as fifteen years ago are increasingly useless.

People frequently ask me if I use an investment advisor for my own investments. I do and I have sought this persons' advice regarding investments and the markets for more than 25 years.

I was fully trained and licensed as a registered representative when I worked in the financial services industry as a young lawyer. I have practiced law in and around the financial markets for forty years. I have taught finance and microeconomics at a respected business school. I have helped to create more than 150 investment securities and I have litigated over several hundred others. As I approach retirement I honestly believe that I could structure my own investment portfolio to help pay my monthly bills.

At the same time, I am smart enough to know that the financial markets are larger, more global and much more complex than at any time since I began working in the financial services industry in the 1970s. **I do know that there is a great deal about the financial markets today that I do not know**.

When people tell me that they are managing a couple of million dollars of their own retirement funds by themselves through a discount brokerage firm, I shudder. If you do manage your own portfolio, ask yourself: *do you really know what you are doing?*

Despite all of the data, all of the analytics, all of the very intelligent and dedicated people who work very hard toward this goal, there is no crystal ball. But some people will manage your money better than others.

Before you begin interviewing investment advisors, there are some things that you should have clear in your own mind. We are past the point of looking at what your retirement needs are or what your retirement dreams may be. We are only looking at your money and how much it might earn. Do the math.

If you have a million dollars and the advisor believes that he could invest your portfolio to produce income at a rate of 6% ($60,000 per year, $5000 per month), then I would call this your baseline number.

Will this amount, together with social security or a pension or other payments that you may receive after you retire, cover your actual expenses? If it does, you may reasonably decide to make those investments and get on with your retirement.

If you make these same investments paying 6% every year and continue to work for three more years, your account will grow almost 20% to $1.2 million and your monthly checks would be almost $6000 per month. If you can obtain a 7% return using liquid investments, the cumulative effect of the reinvestment will continue to work even more in your favor.

Before you start interviewing investment advisors, at least have some idea of the monthly base income that you could obtain with income-producing investments. You should decide how much more you would like to have and how much you can afford to lose to achieve that goal.

The advisor I use for my own investments is independent and personally researches every investment that he buys for his clients. That is primarily the service that I need, someone to select and monitor the investments that will give me income to pay my bills when I slow down or stop working.

My advisor has been managing other peoples' money for a long time. In my opinion, in the money management business there is absolutely no substitute for long-term (multiple market cycle) experience. I have met many of his other clients because they have been with him for many years. How can that ever be a bad thing?

Many of the people that I have referred to this advisor were clients who came to me because another advisor whom they had trusted had betrayed that trust and had caused them to lose a lot of money. These were clients for whom I brought arbitration claims. They were people who felt financially secure when they had retired at the age of 65 and who woke up at age 72 with half as much money or less.

These people were forced to ask: ***where do I go from here and who can I trust?*** I sent them to my advisor because I knew they would need someone who would make them comfortable and earn back their trust.

Call me old-fashioned, but I honestly believe that my advisor cares about me and his other customers. If I did not honestly believe that, I would consider taking my business elsewhere.

These are the traits that I looked for when I first selected my investment advisor. I doubt that you will find a similar list from the industry or the "experts."

1) I wanted to hire a good advisor—not a good salesmen. I wanted to meet and get to know the person who would be making the investment decisions for my money. I wanted to be able to ask questions about the markets, the economy and the investments that he was buying for me. I wanted someone with much more than a superficial understanding of what they were doing.

2) I wanted an advisor who was smart, analytical and aware. Someone who understands the *why* of what they are doing, not just someone going through the motions. I do not want an advisor who parrots research reports to me; I want an advisor who understands the research and who can put the reports into context so that I can understand them as well.

I definitely wanted an advisor who appreciates that the financial markets are becoming more global and more complex. I do not necessarily want to invest in international markets but I do want my advisor to be aware of international competition and markets, especially as it may affect the companies he is considering as a place to invest my money.

3) I wanted an advisor with more than a few years of experience successfully managing other people's money. Would I hire a well-schooled and well-trained advisor who was still young? No. Everyone needs to be trained to manage other people's money. I wanted someone who has also experienced the good and bad times in the markets as well.

Here's a suggested interview question: *what did you learn from the crash in 1987, the tech wreck in 2000 and the credit meltdown in 2008?* I would want to know if the advisors' customers experienced significant losses. If they did and the answer did not include some indication that each crash had changed the way the advisor looked at the numbers or their perspective on the markets, then I would look for someone else. Managing other people's money is much more than what you learn in school.

4) I wanted to have a clear idea of what the advisor would do to limit my losses if the advisor was wrong. Not all strategies work all of the time; markets can be very unpredictable. I do not mind taking some risks, but I do not want to worry about significant losses. Risks can be mitigated and losses limited. I want my advisor to have a plan to protect me. I wanted to know the plan for the "what if" before I invested my first dollar.

5) I wanted an advisor who was independent. Wealth management was at one time almost the exclusive province of large banks and trust companies. People at the top of the business pyramid earned enough to meet the minimum requirements for money management at those firms. Advisors who work for banks or large financial firms today have largely become institutionalized.

My advisor, because he is independent, will never face a sales quota, never be directed to select one fund or investment over another and will never be wedded to research that comes only from the firm at which he works. My advisor works for himself and he works for me.

6) I wanted an advisor who will keep it simple. In many fields of endeavor the more you attempt to accomplish, the more that can go wrong. I wanted a portfolio that would generate income from interest and dividend-producing investments over the long-term. I do not need options, derivatives, international stocks or managed futures. I certainly do not need private placements. I do not want to spend hours going over my monthly statement (which I do review every month). I want to understand what is going on in my account and I want to understand the *why* behind what I see in my statement.

7) I wanted my advisor to be articulate. I am quite knowledgeable about my investments and the conversations that I have with my advisor about them are rarely superficial. Realistically, I will die at some point and one of my children will be faced with the problem of making decisions about the account. I have seen surviving spouses who could not turn their attention to the investment account for months because they were grieving. When they did, they had no idea what they were looking at.

I wanted to make certain that my advisor was articulate enough so that that my children would get the information that they would need to make those decisions in a way that they could understand and be comfortable. It does not cost any more to find an advisor that understands that intangible things like communications skills can be important. I am confident that my advisor could explain these investments to my children and advise them when the need arises.

8) I wanted an investment advisor who worked on a solid, inexpensive platform. There are a great many ways in which a brokerage firm can profit when an advisory account is on its books. Along with an independent advisor, I wanted one who used one of the larger firms as a platform that competes for independent advisors, like Schwab or TD Ameritrade.

I wanted to know that my money was safe and accessible. I wanted to know that any paperwork I might need is online and easy to complete. I like to go online and follow my investments or the market whenever I wish.

9) I wanted to deal with a professional. I wanted an investment advisor who would return my phone calls when I made them and who would be prepared to answer my questions when I asked them. I am a lawyer. I assure you that I could be a pain-in-the-ass customer. With my advisor, I have never had to be. He always does what you would expect a professional to do.

10) I wanted an advisor whom I could trust. It is cliché and I know that blindly trusting an investment advisor because of their reputation or group affinity can be a recipe for disaster.

I trust my advisor because he has earned my trust. I trust that he will ask me the right questions and use my answers to my benefit. I trust my advisor in the same way that I trust the other professionals whose services I engage: my doctors, lawyers and accountant.

I trust that he knows what he is doing because he has always been able to explain what he is doing to me. I trust that, as regards these funds, he is always watching my back.

I feel fortunate that I found the advisor that I have and that I found him so long ago. If you would like to contact him, send me an email and I will send you his contact information. If enough people inquire, I will give him a click-through on my website.

At the end of the day it is not the advisor's prior track record that will matter to you and certainly not how your account performed against a benchmark. What you will care about is the most simple metric—profit and loss. How much money you had when the advisor began to manage your funds versus how much money that you have in the account today, minus how much money you have taken out.

If your advisor is making money for you, I do not see why you would be looking for another. You can always yell "stop" at any time and if you are ahead, so much the better.

If your account suffers losses that you did not anticipate, it is the fact that you did not anticipate the losses that is the problem. If you did not clearly understand that you might lose as much as you did before you began, the advisor did not do their job correctly and I recommend that you seek out another firm.

If your advisor tells you that the *market caused the loss* or that no one saw this negative market action coming or that you should *stay the course* because the *market will recover,* remind them that you hired them to manage your account in good markets and in bad ones. Managing your account should mean more than just letting the market do its thing.

Are you ready for a little financial role-play?

CHAPTER XV

A Fiduciary Investors' Playbook

I offer some financial role-play for readers who are managing their own retirement portfolio of $1 to $5 million or more at discount stockbrokerage firms. If you feel that you are competent to manage that much of your own money, then I would suggest that you would have more than a cursory knowledge about investing and about the financial markets.

I am going to ask you to pretend that you have been asked to join the investment committee that oversees the $100 million endowment fund of a local charity. The charity wants to hire an investment advisory firm to manage those funds. The committee would like your input on which firm to hire.

You know that as a member of the investment committee to an endowment you are likely to be held to a fiduciary's standard of care. You will want to put the funds to work and get a reasonable return to fund the charity's good works.

At the same time, you will want to be certain that the charity is not positioning itself to take on an inappropriate amount of risk or to sustain the significant loss of its funds. All that is expected of you is that you act how a reasonable and prudent investor would act.

The advisory firm that you will help select will actually manage the funds. You just need to formulate some intelligent questions and help choose between the candidates. To help you along, below I will suggest some questions that I would ask.

Many banks, trust companies, stockbrokerage firms, investment advisors, mutual funds and insurance companies will be happy to accept the job. Several will be making presentations to the committee. Glossy brochures, testimonials and unbridled optimism (especially about their own performance) are nice, but should not be factors in the committee's decision. How would you help to select the best firm for the charity to hire?

Let me first warn you that the hardest part of your job may be evaluating advisors who already have a relationship with the charity, especially if they are large donors or supporters. I came across one advisor who donated to one particular charity and who helped them raise money by sponsoring fundraising events every year. The latter allowed him to rub elbows other large donors some of whom became customers of his advisory firm. Ultimately, the charity felt obligated to allow him to manage their money because he had done so much for them. Was he the best advisor they could have found? Was he any good at all?

The lawyer in me would tell you that the first thing the committee should do is review all of the mandatory filings and disclosures that each firm will supply to you. The investment committee will want to satisfy itself that any advisor it considers is properly licensed and appropriately staffed to fulfill its contract.

The official disclosure documents do not say very much about how the money will actually be invested. These disclosures are frequently written by lawyers who do not necessarily know very much about the nuts and bolts of portfolio management.

What passes for mainstream portfolio management is mediocre, at best. There are more professional portfolio managers who get average or below average results than there are superstars who get better results for their customers. Investing and portfolio management require research and statistical analysis. The people who will actually perform these tasks will probably not be the same people who will make a presentation to the committee.

The number crunchers are the people who are actually responsible for your portfolio's success. These are the people whose methods, credentials and experience you are hiring. These are the people whose methods should be at the focus of your review.

I think that it is important for the committee to understand what an advisor intends to do with the charity's money with some specificity. The committee would be well-advised to ask each firm to have a knowledgeable representative walk the committee through the investment process at their firm.

Ask each to explain how they choose the investments that they buy. Ask how they determine when to sell a position. The more details that you get, the better the committee will be able to evaluate and compare the various candidates. I would be skeptical of any firm unwilling to divulge their current holdings and be more likely to hire a firm willing to be more transparent.

Everyone knows that an advisor's past performance is no guarantee of future results. Notwithstanding, the sales pitch for any advisor will likely tout their track record. If the track record that you are given is not audited, I would ask: why not?

It would not be uncommon for the committee to be presented with results for the entire wealth management department of a bank or stockbrokerage firm or a specific investment program within the institution only to find out that the managers whose results you are looking at are not the people who will actually be managing the endowment's funds.

Find out who will be actually managing the charity's money. Take names and investigate these people separately.

Sometimes individual investment advisors or small groups of advisors at a large institution can act independently of the firm and of each other; sometimes they cannot. Many firms do not like the idea of paying research analysts to represent the institution's view of the market or of a particular company and allow their own salespeople to question what their analysts are saying.

As you review an advisor's past performance, I recommend that you focus on years when the overall markets did not do well, such as 2001 or 2008. You would do well to ask an advisor how they performed in difficult markets. Not every advisor's clients lost money in those years and some lost less than others.

Ask the advisor what they think that they did right or wrong during those periods. If they lost money for their customers then, ask what they are doing differently now.

An investment advisor seeking a $100 million account will usually **benchmark** their performance. This is a way for advisors to essentially grade their own performance against how a broad market index, such as the S&P 500 performs. Benchmarking is part of the sale pitch.

The charity could invest in mutual funds or ETFs that also track the index without using the services of an investment advisor. The advisor only adds value by promising to do better than the index every year. The implication of the sales pitch is that they can.

In any event, benchmarking is not an exact science. Each index is intended to represent the market segment that it reflects—but is not perfect. An index is not just a list of stocks whose share prices are accumulated and tracked. Indexes are structured and weighted by the company that prepares them.

Logic suggests that an advisor whose performance is better than the index' performance might be taking higher risks than the average risk of the index. This might not necessarily be true if the advisor was investing in the better companies in the index to the exclusion of the weaker ones. That is why getting the details from each advisor is important.

Understand that benchmarking is also a way in which an advisor can tell you that their management is successful, even if you lose money. If the S&P 500 goes down by 10% in the next twelve months but your account is only down by 8%, the advisor will tell you that your account "beat the benchmark."

There are several ways to look at it but a discussion of benchmarking should necessarily lead to the subject of losses.

The committee should not want or expect any significant losses in a fiduciary account no matter what the market or the benchmarked index does. A broad stock index could go down 20% or more in a year. An advisor trying to beat the index might lose 25% or more. The committee should think twice before it allows an investment advisor to position the account to lose that much of the charity's endowment.

The committee should expect an advisor to have a policy in place to limit or mitigate losses. Some advisors place stop-losses, others hedge in various ways. If an advisor has no strategy to limit losses if the market "corrects," I would look for one that does.

Now that the committee has heard the sales pitch and looked at some general considerations, I suggest that we get down to business and hire the number crunchers that we need.

Step One: Identify the charities' income needs and satisfy them separately. The charity's operations may be funded in various ways including fundraising and grants. If the endowment fund is expected to contribute to the operating budget or fund specific grants, it would be appropriate to invest a portion of the account into income-producing investments to satisfy that need.

This would be the same for an individual investing a retirement or post-retirement account, or a large pension fund balancing contributions with benefit payments. Each must generate enough income to cover withdrawals. Dissipating the endowment's principal to pay the charity's bills cannot be sustained over a long-term.

If the purpose of this fund is to provide some amount towards the operating budget or specific grants, then the logical place to begin a substantive discussion with each candidate would be with questions about potential yields and how they would be achieved. If, for example, it is determined that the endowment fund will contribute $50,000 a month toward the charity's operations or $500,000 per year for scholarships or grants, then a portion of the endowment fund should be segregated to be invested in income-producing investments that would yield at least that amount.

How much the endowment will need to segregate will depend upon the current yields available in the market. Higher yields are always available but will come with higher risks.

Traditionally, a financial advisor to a charitable endowment might have offered a portfolio of investment-grade bonds to provide income. The firm would have charged the endowment a *markup or spread* when it purchased each bond for the account. As the positions were virtually static, many advisors would charge a reduced fee on fixed income investments within a larger portfolio.

Today, there are many types of income-producing investments available that might be suitable for the endowment. I would recommend that the committee ask all candidates how they would construct an appropriate portfolio of income-producing investments to fund the charity's needs.

Assume that the charity's investment committee decides to withdraw $2 million per year from the endowment toward operating expenses. It might be appropriate for the committee to suggest that $40 million be set aside and invested at an average yield of 6%, if that yield was available. The account would generate a little more than needed as an accumulating reserve.

The portion of the portfolio that has not been specifically segregated to provide income will be invested in a diversified portfolio of high-quality equities for long-term growth. We would expect the advisor to construct a portfolio of companies that are solid today, but which are likely to be larger in the future. We would expect the advisor to buy and hold these stocks in the portfolio for a while because a company is not likely to get that much bigger overnight.

Step Two: Locate where you are in the economic cycle. Asset allocation and diversification reduce long-term portfolio risks. As this is a charity's account and we are fiduciaries working on its behalf, it would be foolish not to utilize both of these mainstream strategies to reduce the risk of a substantial loss.

Historically, both the US stock and bond markets have been cyclical and the cycles have often been counter to each other. On its most basic level asset allocation balances a portfolio between stocks, bonds and cash on a percentage basis. The portfolio is periodically rebalanced as debt and equity markets move in relation to each other.

Here we have predetermined that $40 million of the portfolio will be used to generate income and $60 million is available for a long-term equity portfolio. Unless the charity's income needs change, this portion of the portfolio will remain in stocks and not need to be rebalanced with the income-producing side of the portfolio.

Interest rates, bond yields and borrowing costs are still significant indicators of economic health and market conditions. As financial markets expand and globalize, historic cycles may not continue to act exactly as they have in the past. Market trends, good and bad, still need to be identified and considered as the portfolio is put together and managed over time.

Both asset allocation and diversification are essentially mathematical calculations that need to be applied correctly. In order to apply asset allocation and diversification correctly to reduce portfolio risk in the real world, you must first understand where you are in the real world. Understanding the interrelationship between market sectors, interest rates, commodity prices and international politics is essential to the portfolio's success.

I would ask any candidate what trends they see for both the credit and equity markets for the next 24 months and also for the next five years. What answer am I looking for? The one with the best reasoning behind it, the one that indicates the advisor is aware of broader market conditions and considers them in the investment process.

Step Three: Select the right stock-pickers. At their core, a great many portfolio managers are stock-pickers. They analyze and research various companies and stocks and pick what they believe to be the best investments for their clients. That is the service that these advisors are selling: fundamental securities analysis. It is also what the committee is buying. Some investment advisors do it better than others.

Fundamental analysis became standardized after WWII. It is a process where balance sheet and financial statement items are analyzed and compared against an established series of formulas and ratios. The object is to identify those companies that represent the best investment opportunities—stocks that represent better value than the stocks of their competitors.

Fundamental analysis was the standard when I studied it in college and worked on Wall Street in the 1970s. It was the standard when I taught business school students how to break down a balance sheet to look at a company's fundamentals in the 1990s.

The ratio of a stock's price to its earnings and its earnings per share are widely considered to be the two basic metrics for the analysis of any stock, though far from all that an investor would want to consider.

It was not until the 1970s that the SEC adopted many of the standard forms upon which public companies now report their quarterly and annual financial results. It was even later until companies in other countries adopted financial disclosures that could be accurately compared with disclosures made by companies in the US.

At the time, the stock exchanges were still the primary auction markets. Transactions were made between brokers on the exchange floor who frequently shouted or sent hand signals to each other. Economics taught that rational buyers and sellers set the price of any stock in the marketplace.

In the 1990s, people were just beginning to understand that the financial markets were becoming efficient. An efficient market is one where everyone has the same information about each company at the same time. Everyone can perform the same analysis and take action—to either buy or sell the company's shares—without high cost or difficulty. All information about a company, good and bad, is factored into the price of the stock, which is attributed to the collective wisdom of the various decision makers.

By that standard, markets today are much more efficient than they were in the 1990s. Information is more widely disseminated and access to the markets is easier and cheaper. The number of large, well-informed investors is vastly increased. At the same time, market makers and other middlemen have been eliminated from many transactions, reducing costs and leveling the playing field around the globe.

Ideas about how to invest in an efficient market are still evolving. So much has been deferred to the *collective wisdom of the market* that some people are trying to plot the psychology of market players. Many people see values beyond the balance sheets and work to quantify those values.

What do I mean by that? Before the tech crash in 2000-2001 there was a great deal of money invested in companies that had no products and no sales, nor anything tangible. No amount of fundamental analysis could support those investment decisions.

A lot of people, including a lot of retirees and professional investors, invested anyway. Many of those people took a beating when the market crashed, taking losses on stocks that they had no fundamental reason to buy in the first place.

An unspoken truth about any investment advisor is that when they purchase a stock for their clients' accounts, they always expect that the price of the stock will rise. If the advisor did not think that the price would go up, they would not buy the stock.

That does not mean that any advisor will be right with every purchase. But the collective wisdom does seem to still appreciate and rely upon fundamental securities analysis. I would expect any advisor that the committee would ultimately hire to do the same.

Beyond fundamental analysis, I would want to know that a qualified professional analyst—or more than one—would research every company in the portfolio. Research analysts start with fundamental analysis but also look at a company's management, products, markets, customers, suppliers and competition. None of these will show up on a company's balance sheet but any one may be crucial to a company's success or failure. This takes judgment beyond the balance sheet.

The number crunching does not stop there. Properly diversified, the account will invest in companies operating in fifteen or more diverse sectors of the marketplace.

Into which sectors the endowment's funds should be invested and how the funds will be allocated, sector-to-sector and in individual securities within each sector, is where the account will either succeed or fail.

To correctly diversify a portfolio, it is important to purchase individual stocks that will *correlate* with other stocks in the portfolio. It is one thing to correlate oil companies with an airline as oil prices move, but even that is an imperfect correlation. To do it correctly is no easy task and takes an understanding of mathematics superior to my own.

I do understand that it is difficult to correctly correlate companies one against the other because multinational companies have many suppliers and operate in many markets and in many currencies. There are so many different factors that can affect their business and the performance of their shares that a reasonably precise correlation with other companies may not be possible. That does not mean that I would not expect an investment advisor to include these or other multinational companies in the portfolio.

I would want to know that the sectors into which the portfolio was divided were weighted, taking into consideration real world economic and market conditions. I would then expect them to purchase the best stocks in each sector.

I would hope that the committee would hire an advisor that understands the economics of the marketplace as well as the mathematics of investing. I firmly believe that the endowment needs both to invest successfully.

One question that I would ask each of the candidates is what would they do about international currency risks. It is a trick question, but it is also frequently elicits informative responses.

There are currency risks in the international markets that may be larger than similar risks for domestic companies. Some investment advisors would allocate a portion of the portfolio to international funds so as to capture any profits from this sector, but international stocks are not really a sector any more than large cap or small cap stocks are a market sector for purposes of diversification.

An international stock fund will not correlate with anything else that you have in the portfolio. If an advisor tells you that buying an international fund is intended to enhance a diversification strategy and reduce portfolio risks, it is a clear sign that they do not understand diversification, international markets or currency risks. Adding these risks to the portfolio without a correlated opposite increases the overall risk of the portfolio rather than diminishing it.

If the committee had started with a goal, it would have been fair to express it as follows: to find a portfolio management firm that would create a diversified portfolio across various sectors of the market, weighted according to current market conditions and which purchased the best anticipated performers in each sector.

By now you should appreciate that it takes a lot of math and a lot of number crunching to do it correctly. The winning candidate will certainly be a firm that could crunch the numbers and intelligently interpret the results.

I have written elsewhere that: "If one investment advisory firm was truly better than all of the others and truly made the most money for its clients' year-in and year-out, it would be no secret. The investment committee of every retirement and pension fund (and every charity and endowment) would direct their funds to that firm and that would be that."

The truth is that while researching this book, I was reminded that there probably is one investment advisory firm that would be better than most for this type of fiduciary account.

I have been aware of this firm for at least twenty years. Their reputation is excellent. I attended a presentation by one of their analysts a few years ago and came away impressed. I believe that they would approach the management of the endowment's portfolio in much the same way as I have described. Of late, they have gotten some significant recognition.

I am not in the business of recommending specific investment advisors. If you are actually a fiduciary investor, investing the funds for a group, fund or charity, I will send you the name of this investment advisory firm if you send me an email. They do not compensate me in any way.

You were chosen for this investment committee because you were managing your own portfolio. The object of this role-playing exercise was to get you to look at the nuts and bolts of portfolio construction and management.

Do you separately manage your income-producing investments? Do you understand fundamental analysis? Do you crunch the numbers?

I have asked many people who are managing their own money: *why do you buy the stocks that you buy?* No one professes to have a crystal ball. Very few people actually read quarterly or annual reports.

Most never consider that changes in the credit markets can affect companies, their suppliers and customers differently. Some people follow particular analysts, newsletter publishers, pundits or tipsters that they like. No one can really expect that any one of these experts will be correct a significant part of the time.

When looking at the portfolio through the eyes of a fiduciary, knowing that you need to lower the risk while balancing the risk and return, the approach that I have outlined makes sense. Many professional advisors would agree.

So my question to you is this: *why would you take better care of the charity's money than you do your own?*

Many people manage their own money. Most, in my opinion, are just knowledgeable enough to get themselves into serious trouble.

When I visit my financial advisor during the work day he may have four or five different screens on: a financial news channel, several tickers, special screens for stocks that his clients own, special screens for stocks that he is thinking about but does not yet own and information about client portfolios. He has his eyes on the market all day, every day. Does that describe how you manage your portfolio?

Throughout this book I have tried to keep readers and especially retirees out of financial trouble. If you retired and you are managing more than $1 million of your own money, go back and re-read the chapter on finding a really good financial advisor. Hire a registered investment advisor to do what needs to be done for you.

Final Thoughts

I wrote this book to help people who were investing for their retirement avoid mistakes and miscreants, and to help them see through the hype and the advertising a little more clearly. (I also wanted to raise a little money for cancer research.)

The money that was invested in the bad scams and bad strategies I described had taken people a lifetime to accumulate. It was the money that they needed to pay their bills when they stopped working. It was the money that they needed to pay for medical care if they get sick as they get older.

Financial professionals who steer customers to scam artists necessarily erode investors' trust in the financial markets. They also divert hundreds of billions of dollars of capital into worthless and inappropriate enterprises.

Just the private placements issued by Medical Capital, DBSI and Provident Royalties represent $3.5 billion in securities sales that should not have been made because the offerings were fraudulent. They are the tip of a large iceberg.

Financial professionals are required to investigate the securities that they are selling and should be able to backup any claims that are being made. These sales and hundreds of billions of dollars of similar sales would not have been made if anyone had thoroughly investigated the investments first.

There is a lot of bad investment advice out there. A lot of it is mainstream and so ingrained in the system that even regulators believe it. Some of it can really set you on a path that will lead to significant investment losses. Some of the advice is just plain foolish if you consider that it does not really help anyone at all.

Here are two things that government and consumer groups will tell you to do to avoid bad investments. They are not so much foolish, as not really likely to protect you from very much.

1) Investigate before you invest. This is never bad advice. However, the two largest offending investments—private placements and variable annuities—cannot really be investigated by the average investor. Most investors who own them are not capable of reading the small print that accompanies these products, let alone understand it. They would not know where to begin to investigate these financial products. If you become aware that the person who is selling this investment to you has not investigated it either, how do you know if what you are being told about the investment is true?

2) Investigate your salesperson. This is not bad advice either. I refer people to the Broker-Check® system because it is the best system around. Broker-Check was intended to track serious complaints that customers make against stockbrokers. Clearly, the worst brokers should have the most complaints. Not so.

FINRA, the securities industry group that established this program, allows brokers to buy their way out of the reporting process. Dozens of complaints against stockbrokers that I have personally filed in the last ten years have been expunged and show up nowhere in the system. Those complaints are never reported to prospective customers. Therefore, you cannot expect the Broker-Check system to report all serious complaints that may have been made against a stockbroker.

The sales pitch that you will hear will always tell you that *you need more money* and *you can have more money.* In advertising parlance these are referred to as *fear and greed,* two of the most powerful emotional triggers that will cause people to act.

They are the mainstay of the financial services industry. I should not have to tell you that making an emotional decision about something as important as your retirement investments is never a good idea.

If you spend your life putting away money to have when you retire, then the first thing that you should think about when you retire is conserving that money. The problem is that a great many people earn significant commissions and fees to direct your money into investments that are *not* designed to conserve your funds.

Investing is essentially a mathematical process that requires analysis of every individual investment that you make and an understanding of the greater economy in which the investment exists. Even the best of the best do not always get it right.

You should not use that as an excuse to not utilize the best methods or to consult with the best people as regards retirement investing. That does not necessary mean people who work at the largest firms.

Let me offer some thoughts of my own. I assure you that this is not a list that you will see anywhere else.

1) The most important retirement investment tool for many people may be a mirror. Look into one and see yourself. Picture your life after you retire. What do you want? What can you afford?

The latter is a question that you have asked and answered all of your life. Retirement living is no different. Start with a real expense budget. Do not let anyone tell you that you will be spending twice as much in any one year no matter how long you live.

2) If it is safety first, then it is safety first. If you make it to retirement with a fair amount of savings and the prospect of being able to pay your bills for the rest of your life, even if you need to cut back a little, why muck it up?

If are seduced by higher returns, you are going to be taking on extra risks. There is nothing wrong and everything right about asking yourself: do you really, truly, want that extra risk?

If the salesperson tells you that an investment is safe and suitable for retirees, be careful. The only investments that a financial professional is permitted to call *safe* are US Treasury securities and some other government bonds.

3) Do not give into the hype. Do not let yourself become seduced by the "we can get you more" crowd. In the financial markets the best way to get more is to risk more.

The higher the financial reward that you are trying to achieve, the greater the chance that you will end up with less money. If you end up with a lot less money ten or fifteen years after you retire, you are likely to be in trouble.

4) Keep it simple. People are always amazed when I tell them that they could have gotten a 6% or 7% return without all of the bells, whistles, paperwork, risk and grief that they went through. Offsetting risks or hedging them is not the same as not taking them.

An investment that has a high return with limited risk is the Holy Grail of investing. If someone discovered how to create one, the news would get out.

5) Ask about commissions and fees; they are paid with your money. In the real world people do not buy investments; other people are paid to sell them. The truly high-risk investments, private placements and variable annuities, which should rarely be offered to seniors or retirees, pay the highest sales commission.

If the financial professional with whom you deal refuses to tell you how much they are earning from your investments or tells you that commission is included in your purchase, go elsewhere.

6) Financial and investment fraud is widespread and growing. Be careful and be diligent about your finances and the people you are trusting to provide you with investment advice. Be especially leery of unsolicited calls urging you to invest in the next hot thing. If something sounds too good to be true it probably is.

7) Use common sense. Take a step back and ask yourself why the great investment in front of you is not being scooped up by investors more savvy than you. Ask yourself: what could go wrong with this investment? Ask yourself: what are you going to do if it does?

8) Follow your gut. Unfortunately, many people who sell financial products and advice are less than honest and constantly tantalized with larger commissions for selling the products fewer people should want. I have heard people describe financial salespeople as *secretive, evasive, slick, oily* and *unctuous* – and remarkably turned their money over to them anyway.

You do not have to love your financial professional, but if you are not completely comfortable there may be a good reason.

9) Hire a number cruncher. You really need investment advice from someone who can do the math. Investing is a mathematical process that requires more data than most people would think, especially in today's large global economy. If you hire an investment advisor to help you, and I recommend that you do, it is not that difficult to separate the number crunchers from everyone else.

10) Ask a lot of questions and never take your eye off of the ball. A good salesperson will have answers for the top ten questions that you may potentially ask. Ask them anyway. Continue to review your investments and account every month and continue to ask specific questions about the expectations for every purchase and why that purchase was right for you.

I firmly believe that you can find the right person to set up your investment portfolio and to manage it for you. You should be able to achieve a reasonable return on your investments without taking on inordinate risk.

I hope that some people will take the advice that I have offered and not make some of the mistakes that I have outlined.

I hope you all enjoy being retired.

Acknowledgements

For more than 20 years I worked with an outstanding group of people representing investors filing claims in securities industry arbitration forums. Richard and Tanya Sacks, Tim Canning and the late Jim Sullivan were the nucleus of a team of which I consider myself fortunate to have been a part. We supported each other, learned from each other and helped a great many people recover their investment losses.

This book was made possible by a wonderful professional named Ruth Schwartz. She calls herself a book mid-wife but book-magician would be a better description. She took my manuscript and turned it into the book that you see here. If I had not found her, it would not have happened.

About the Author

Irwin Stein is a Wall Street-trained attorney who has practiced law in and around the capital markets for 40 years. He has represented top-of-the-line investment banks and some of Wall Street's more infamous scoundrels. Over the years he has helped many companies raise funds to start or expand their business.

For the last 20 years he has worked with a group representing investors who were defrauded by financial sharks and mainstream financial firms and advisors. This book recounts some of those cases. It is intended to help investors, especially baby boomers who are about to retire, avoid some of the same costly mistakes.

Mr. Stein's practice was interrupted in 2011 when he was diagnosed with leukemia. All proceeds that he receives from the sale of this book will be donated to cancer research. He staunchly opposes the idea that he is a cancer survivor, preferring to be called a cancer conquistador instead.

Mr. Stein taught Economics, Law and Economics, Finance and related courses at Golden Gate University in San Francisco for most of the 1990s. Visit his blog at laweconomicscapital.com or contact him at Profstein18@yahoo.com or through LinkedIn.

Printed in Dunstable, United Kingdom

91222381R00107